KID ON PURPOSE

A JOURNEY TO WHOLEHEARTED CHILDHOOD

SARAH HER

To the child who dares to do great things.
I believe in you.

And to my husband.
For believing in me.

Kid on Purpose
Copyright © 2020 by Sarah Her
ISBN 978-0-578-74608-1

Disclaimer: This book was inspired by Rick Warren's work, *The Purpose Driven Life*. However, it and its author do not propose to be nor are associated with, supported or endorsed by Rick Warren or the Purpose Driven brand.

"You are young, but do not let anyone treat you as if you were not important. Be an example to show the believers how they should live. Show them with your words, with the way you live, with your love, with your faith, and with your pure life."

1 Timothy 4:12 ICB

CONTENTS

Activities

ACKNOWLEDGMENTS

K. Day
J. Hunter
Y. Kue
B. Kugel
K. Lao
T. Lor
S. Lor
N. Olson
J. Schueler
R. Thorpe
T. Scott
A. Vang
A. Yang
Z. Yang

Kid on Purpose can serve its purpose because of you. Thank you.

A NOTE TO CAREGIVERS

Dear grown-up,

Thank you for showing up for the small things, the day-to-day things, the why-did-I-agree-to-this things. Thank you for saying "yes" to your kiddos. This is where it starts: With your heart being in the right place.

So again, from the bottom of my heart: Thank you for showing up.

You're living in a time where families and the people in those families are busier than they've ever been--ever. You work and run errands. You commit to loved ones, ministry, play dates, sports and countless other things. You're in charge of managing the health, ongoing development and overall wellness for both you and the children you're raising. Every. Single. Day. And on top of all that, God's calling you to lead your kids' spiritual formation.

That's a tough gig.

Kid on Purpose is here to help you succeed with the latter. This book is crafted to take kids ages 6-12 on a spiritual formation journey through short and meaningful devotionals. It's also designed with you in mind: your guidance will help form your children's view of God, themselves and the world. You'll shape how they relate to their heavenly Father, understand their individuality and contribute to God's story. You'll lead the spiritual formation of your kids--by simply showing up and saying, "Yes, Lord."

There'll be days completing the devotional is going to feel like an impossible feat and days you'll get lost in an activity. From grown-up to grown-up: Every exposure to Jesus is worth it. Most importantly, you are worthy of this calling. All God needs is your willingness. He's at work as you offer up your time and energy, growing every seed you sow and water. They will bear good fruit.

I'm praying for you and your family. God bless you with everything you need to lead your children.

Sincerely,

Sarahey

PREPARING FOR YOUR JOURNEY

HOW TO USE THIS WORKBOOK

This workbook has 40 devotionals that will take your kids on a journey to understand why God made them and what he wants to do with their lives. It's an important and often hard journey. Find friends and grown-ups you and your young ones trust to go with you.

The journey is split into 6 parts, each with a different theme: Purpose, Worship, Fellowship, Discipleship, Ministry and Evangelism. They're outlined on page **vii**.

Each part is structured the same way:

- The first chapter of each part introduces the theme
- The middle chapters take a closer look at what the theme means
- The last chapter reviews what's been learned that week

Each devotional has 5 parts: **Know**, **Read**, **Think**, **Pray** and **Do**. These sections are explained on the next page.

KNOW

Know lists the Big Question, Big Idea and memory verse for the week. Big Questions are questions a lot of people ask at some point in their life. People have been asking them for thousands of years because finding the answers to them isn't easy or fast. Your kiddos might have even asked you these questions before.

Big Ideas are biblical answers to Big Questions. They may sound simple, but most people will spend an entire lifetime asking God and other Christians for guidance on how to live them out every day.

"Know" also provides a Bible passage. Verses highlighted in the "Read" section come from the listed reference. Read the whole story behind the excerpt to get the most out of the devotional.

READ

While not labeled in the devotionals, Read comprises the bulk of each one. It talks about the aspects behind the Big Idea, emphasizing it in different ways each day with the hope that your kiddos will have a deeper understanding of the Big Idea by the end of the week. Except for days on which kiddos "Get to Know the Big Idea" and "Make the Big Idea Personal," each section features a Bible verse. Bible verses are highlighted with colored text. Their references can be found in the "Passage" line of the "Know" section.

THINK

Think prompts your children to reflect on and respond to what they've read. It takes them a step further from thinking about the reading to applying it to their lives.

PRAY

Pray leads your children in a conversation with God about the specific topic brought up in the devotional that day. You and your kids can talk about or add to the prayer to make it more personal.

<u>Do</u> presents an activity that gives you and your kids a chance to further experience the Big Idea. Lead them in joining faith and action!

QUICK TIP

If you run into a word you or your kids don't know, take a moment to look it up and explain it. To get the most out of this experience, complete each devotional in its entirety and explore questions as they come up.

All parts of this book work together to give you and your kiddos a whole–person approach to learning about God's purposes for them as *individuals* and as *members of his family.*

As you and your young ones work through *Kid on Purpose*, I encourage you to pour into your kids and allow your kids to pour into you. Share with them what's on your heart and ask them what's going on in theirs. Chances are you'll take turns learning from one another as you go, which will make this journey all the more rewarding. No activity in this book (or any book!) can replace heart–to–heart, face–to–face time with your kids.

WORKBOOK OUTLINE

Week 1 (Days 1–7): Purpose
» Big Question: What am I doing here?
» Big Idea: I was made *on* purpose, *for* a purpose.
» Bible Verse: Ephesians 2:10 NIV

• •

Week 2 (Days 8–14): Worship
» Big Question: What does God want from me?
» Big Idea: I'm made to love God
» Bible Verse: Mark 12:30 NIV

• •

Week 3 (Days 15–21): Fellowship
» Big Question: Where do I belong?
» Big Idea: I'm made for God's family
» Bible Verse: Romans 12:5 NIV

• •

Week 4 (Days 22–28) Discipleship
» Big Question: What kind of person do I want to be?
» Big Idea: I'm made to become like Christ
» Bible Verse: Philippians 2:5 NIV

• •

Week 5 (Days 29–35): Ministry
» Big Question: What should I do with my life?
» Big Idea: I'm made to serve God
» Bible Verse: 1 Peter 4:10 NIV

• •

Week 6 (Days 36–40): Evangelism
» Big Question: How can my life make a difference?
» Big Idea: I'm made to do my part
» Bible Verse: Colossians 4:5 NIV

THE BEGINNING

The story you belong to started before the universe existed, back when there was only God. He was (and still is!) full of splendor and power. He wanted to show his might, so the world you know began (John 1:3).

God spun galaxies, hung stars and shaped planets. He spoke flying creatures and swimming critters to life. He breathed life into humans.

He filled the whole world with goodness. The best part? He gave it all to you (Genesis 1–2).

God is perfect. That means he's 100% *good*. His thoughts, words and actions are honest, true and pure. He wants to help, not harm.

Because of his goodness, he made a perfect home for everything he created. There was no sadness in this home. No fear or loneliness. No rejection or failure. No brokenness. All of creation lived in peace.

But this perfect home didn't last long.

Sin entered our hearts: now we had selfish thoughts, said hurtful words and acted in nasty ways. We had to leave our perfect home, where only perfect people could live (Genesis 3).

Our world was broken, and there was no way we could fix it (Isaiah 43:11).

But God could. In fact, he can do anything he wants (Matthew 19:26)! So he came up with an amazing plan to heal the brokenness in our world (like pollution) and in our hearts (like selfishness).

You see, even though we're sinners, God still loves us (Romans 5:8). He still wants us to be part of his family.

Becoming a part of it is a challenge, though: God is perfect and anyone who wants to be in his family also has to be perfect (that means no breaking the rules--ever!).

WALKING
ONLY

We're sinners (Romans 3:10); we definitely don't make the cut.

Once we saw how ~~hard~~ impossible it is to be perfect, we knew we were in big trouble (Romans 3:23). None of our plans were making us perfect. We hurt God and others every day. And we can't stop (no matter how much we try). There was no way we could be part of God's family.

Until Jesus came along (Romans 3:23–25).

God's amazing plan to heal brokenness isn't about us trying to heal our world and our hearts. It's about Jesus healing the brokenness (Ephesians 2:8–9) and showing us how to get to God (John 14:6).

Jesus is way more powerful than we are. He's 100% good––like God. He was the perfect man for rescuing broken people––like us.

Jesus knew that only perfect people get to be part of God's family. There's no room for brokenness in his perfect home. He also knew the only ending for anyone who isn't part of God's family is death (Romans 6:23).

Jesus didn't want death to be the end of our story. And he knew the only way sinners could ever join God's family was if a perfect person traded his perfection for their sin––by dying for them.

As scary as dying can be, Jesus thought about how much he loves broken people. He loved them enough to leave his Father and home in heaven (John 6:38). He loved them enough to come to earth and live with them in their messy homes and dirty streets (John 1:14).

Jesus loved broken people so much that he wasn't afraid of any unknown, even if the unknown was death (John 3:16). So he made a choice that changed the world.

He chose to die for broken people (Romans 5:6–8). He died once and he died for all––the sinners in the Bible and the ones around today (Hebrews 10:10, 14). Jesus shared his perfection with us so we, too, could be perfect. So we, too, could have the chance to be healed and live in a healed world with a God who loves us to the moon and back (Hebrews 9:26–28). Forever (Romans 8:38–39).

The day Jesus died was the saddest day the world had ever seen. God's heart broke (Matthew 27:45–46); his son was dead (Matthew 27:50). But both he and Jesus knew it had to happen this way if they wanted to have what they wanted most: you (John 3:17).

Three days after Jesus' death, the rest of their rescue plan unfolded for the world to see: Jesus rose from the dead (Mark 16:1–7). He had gone to the darkness, defeated Satan and come back to life (Hebrews 2:14). He showed everyone how powerful he is and what he would do to give sinners a chance to be part of his family.

You can't stop sinning. Jesus knows this, so he lived a 100% good life for you. Then he traded your sin for his 100% goodness (1 John 2:2). He took death meant for sinners and gave you eternal life meant for perfect people (Titus 3:5). And now you have a chance to join God's family, be healed and live in a healed world when he returns (Romans 5:10–11).

You can be part of God's family by

1. Admitting you're a sinner and asking God to forgive you

2. Believing that Jesus did all the work for you (since being 100% good 100% of the time is impossible!)

3. Asking the Holy Spirit to teach you how to think, speak and act according to what's right in God's eyes

Did you know that you can join God's family whenever you want to (Romans 10:13)? When you're ready to accept God's invitation into his family (that can be today, next week, or even a long time from now), pray this (Romans 10:9–10):

"Dear God, I'm a sinner and I can't help myself.
I believe you love me; you sent Jesus to die for me.
You've given me a chance to find healing
by being part of your family.
I want to be part of your family.
Forgive me for sinning. Please live with me.
Change my thoughts, words and actions
so that everyone around me can see
how great your love is.
In Jesus' name, amen."

God's heard your heart–felt prayer (1 John 1:9)! Now he wants to help you make the most of your life. You can do that by loving God, following Jesus' example and sharing the good news (Romans 8:1) of his love to the world around you. This book will teach you how to do those things. By the end of this journey, you'll be a force to be reckoned with: a kid on purpose (Matthew 18:2–6)!

MY PROMISE

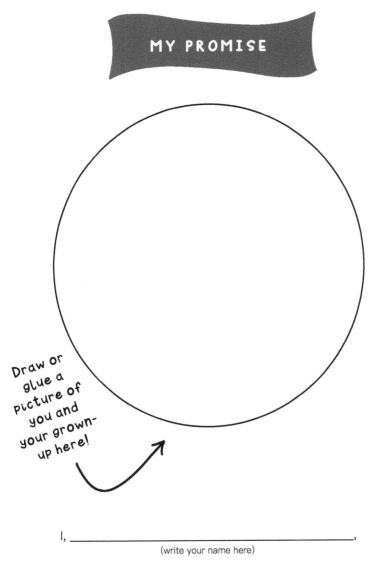

Draw or glue a picture of you and your grown-up here!

I, _____,
(write your name here)

promise to learn as much as I can about God's purpose for my life
and his family in the next 40 days.

I, _____,
(write your grown-up's name here)

promise to help this kiddo learn as much as they can about God's
purpose for their life and his family in the next 40 days.

_____
(write the day you start your journey here)

PART 1: PURPOSE

I was made on purpose, for a purpose

Get to Know the Big Idea: Purpose

KNOW

Big Question: What am I doing here?

Big Idea: I was made on purpose, for a purpose

Bible Verse: "For we are God's workmanship, created in Christ Jesus to do good works, which God prepared in advance for us to do." Ephesians 2:10 NIV

Did you know that God was getting ready for your arrival even before your grown-ups found out you were on the way?

Whether they knew you were coming or not, God made you *on purpose* (that means he wanted you here) and he made you *for a purpose* (that means you've got a special job to do!).

You're exactly what God had in mind when he made you!

God created you and gave you all sorts of gifts (things you're naturally good at) and passions (things you care a lot about). God loves you so much.

He made you to love him back, too. You can use your thoughts, words, and actions to show him and the people around you that you love him. When you do that, you live out your purpose!

THINK

Believing God loves you can be hard.

1. What does God do to show he loves you?

2. What does God's love feel like?

3. Who else shows you God's love?

PRAY

Dear God, thank you for planning my life and giving it a purpose. I want to do what you created me to do! Help me discover my gifts and passions. Show me how to love you with my thoughts, my words, and my actions.

DO

You were made for God to love and enjoy. Read about what he's like in Revelation 1:12–15. Then draw a picture of him on the next page.

My Drawing of God

You're Where You're Supposed to Be

Have you heard of Joseph? He had 12 brothers who didn't like him very much because he was their dad's favorite child. They sold Joseph into slavery then lied to their father about what happened to him (they told him Joseph was eaten by a wild animal).

Joseph was taken from his family, but he wasn't alone: He had God. God was with Joseph and Joseph never stopped trusting God. Years later, Joseph would become Pharaoh's right hand man and save the people of the land (including his brothers) from famine.

Joseph said to his brothers, "You planned to harm me. But God planned it for good. He planned to do what is now being done. He wanted to save many lives."

KNOW

Big Question: What am I doing here?

Big Idea: I was made on purpose, for a purpose.

Bible Verse: "For we are God's workmanship, created in Christ Jesus to do good works, which God prepared in advance for us to do." Ephesians 2:10 NIV

Passage: Gen. 37, 39–50 NIRV

In good and bad times, God's love for you remains the same. He's always helping you fulfill his purpose for your life. There's only one catch: like Joseph, you have to trust he's got everything under control and that he'll show you his perfect plan when the time is right.

THINK

God can give each season of life a purpose if you let him.

Name something that's giving you a hard time right now. What might God be trying to teach you?

PRAY

Lord, you're always with me wherever I go. Thanks for staying with me. ____ is giving me a hard time right now. It makes me feel ____. Please bring good things out of this hard experience, and one day, help me see the work you did.

DO

God was with Joseph and helped him fulfill his purpose.

Ask your grown-up to share about a time they waited for God to reveal his perfect plan.

What Do You Live For?

If God said you could have anything you wanted, what would you ask for?

God once asked King Solomon the same question. He led God's people at that time. It was a stressful job. He could have asked for a vacation or new toy to help him relax. Instead, King Solomon asked for "a heart that understands" so that he could "tell the difference between what is right and what is wrong."

King Solomon wanted to be a great leader for God's people. With God's help, he fulfilled that purpose—as the wisest and richest man alive during his time. God told King Solomon, "I will give you a wise and understanding heart . . . And that is not all. I will give you what you have not asked for. I will give you wealth and honor."

King Solomon's purpose was to lead God's people as their king. He knew he'd need help with that, so he asked the best helper of all for support—God! He's ready to equip you to fulfill your purpose. What he wants is your, "Yes!"

THINK

Solomon wanted to rule God's people well, so he asked for wisdom. God equipped him for that purpose.

1. What do you think God wants to do with your life?

2. What do you need to get there?

PRAY

Dear God, you prepare your people to do good things. Help me see what you want for my life. Guide me and send people to help me to fulfill your purpose.

DO

The wisdom God gave King Solomon might not look like what others say it does.

Explore wisdom through God's eyes on the next page.

Finding Wisdom

Read the verse below. Then draw or write how someone with wisdom would respond to each scenario.

Calvin hits his little brother. He wants to apologize for being mean. What would wisdom **sound** like in this case?	Lani sees that her friend is sad. She wants to make her feel better. What would wisdom **feel** like in this case?

"But the wisdom that comes from heaven is pure. That's the most important thing about it. And that's not all. It also loves peace. It thinks about others. It obeys. It is full of mercy and good fruit. It is fair. It doesn't pretend to be what it is not."

James 3:17 NIRV

Mai used her lunch money for new shoes. Her dad asked her where it went. What would wisdom **look** like in this case?	Andre's brother can be mean to him. Andre wants him to be kinder. What would wisdom **sound** like in this case?

Made For Big Things

God's given you unique gifts. He's also put you in a place where you can use those gifts to lead other people into his family.

Esther's gifts were beauty and boldness. She was so beautiful King Xerxes made her his queen. Guided by the wisdom of her cousin, Mordecai, she not only saved the king's life but the lives of her people, the Jews, as well.

When faced with the chance to do what was right, Esther was afraid. She was standing up to the king, after all! Thankfully, Mordecai was there to remind her of God's purpose: "Who knows? It's possible that you became queen for a time just like this."

Esther knew her position as queen was a blessing from God. She knew her purpose was greater than looking pretty next to the king. She said yes to using her gifts for God's purpose——and God used her to save his people from destruction.

God wants to use you to do big things, too! He's got a purpose for your life. Learning to hear and obey him is the first step to completing it.

KNOW

Big Question: What am I doing here?

Big Idea: I was made on purpose, for a purpose.

Bible Verse: "For we are God's workmanship, created in Christ Jesus to do good works, which God prepared in advance for us to do." Ephesians 2:10 NIV

Passage: Esther 2-4, 7-8 NIRV

11

_____

_____

_____

_____

_____

_____

_____

_____

_____

_____

_____

_____

_____

_____

_____

_____

THINK

God used Esther for his purpose because she let him. Act out the answers to the questions below:

1. What are some of your gifts?

2. Who can help you figure out what God's plan for your life is?

PRAY

Lord, I want to serve you like Esther served you. Show me the gifts you've given me and the people you want me to serve. Help me know what's right in your eyes and give me courage to do it.

DO

Most things are created with a purpose in mind (example: toothbrushes are made to clean teeth).

Name 5 things around your house. What's their purpose?

DAY 5

Living Life for God

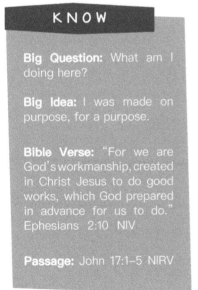

KNOW

Big Question: What am I doing here?

Big Idea: I was made on purpose, for a purpose.

Bible Verse: "For we are God's workmanship, created in Christ Jesus to do good works, which God prepared in advance for us to do." Ephesians 2:10 NIV

Passage: John 17:1–5 NIRV

Jesus came to earth with a plan. He came to do God's will (Jn. 6:48); to experience life as a human (Heb. 2:14–17); to save sinners (1 Tim. 1:15); to destroy the devil (1 Jn. 3:8); and to show you how much God loves you (Jn. 3:16).

Jesus did that and way more, fulfilling God's purpose for his life. He didn't spend any time arguing with God or debating if he wanted to obey or not. He got to know God, understood what God wanted to do with his life and then obeyed.

When you do the work God prepared for you to do, you display his greatness: "I [Jesus] have brought you [God] glory on earth. I have finished the work you gave me to do."

Each time you glorify God by doing the work he's given you to do, you show others how amazing God is and give them a chance to say yes to being part of his amazing plan, too.

13

THINK

Jesus lived for God by using his resources (gifts, relationships, time, energy) to share God's love with others. In the same way, you're in charge of the resources you have.

1. How can you use your time to glorify God?

2. Share about a time you glorified God by doing what's right.

PRAY

Lord God, you've given me different resources to use for your purposes here on earth. I want to show others your love, but it can be hard to do what you want instead of what I want. Change my heart so that I listen to and obey you.

DO

There's no way you can pay Jesus back for what he has done for you. Thankfully, He doesn't ask you to.

Thank him for everything he's done by giving him 10 minutes of your time today. No distractions!

NOTES

_____

_____

_____

_____

_____

_____

_____

_____

_____

_____

_____

_____

_____

_____

_____

_____

_____

_____

_____

_____

Not Made for Brokenness

It only takes a quick look out the window to see that the world is full of brokenness: people hurting nature, one another and themselves. God made you to live forever, but definitely not on earth as it is right now. This may be your home for the time being, but you aren't made for it. You don't belong in a broken world.

One day, God is going to replace your broken world with a perfect one. Everyone in his family will live there; and this time, there will be no way brokenness can enter.

The perfect forever home is still on its way. While you wait, you can learn what your purpose is and live it out. In doing so, the message of God's love will spread. People from all over the earth will have the chance to hear and accept the invitation into his family--an invitation into healing and the best life possible in this broken world.

KNOW

Big Question: What am I doing here?

Big Idea: I was made on purpose, for a purpose.

Bible Verse: "For we are God's workmanship, created in Christ Jesus to do good works, which God prepared in advance for us to do." Ephesians 2:10 NIV

Passage: Hebrews 13:14 ICB

"Here on earth we do not have a city that lasts forever. But we are looking for the city that we will have in the future."

15

NOTES

_____

_____

_____

_____

_____

_____

_____

_____

_____

_____

_____

_____

_____

_____

_____

_____

_____

_____

THINK

It can be heartbreaking living in a broken world. Feeling overwhelmed and hopeless is something everyone experiences.

1. Name something you've seen or heard that's broken your heart.

2. What can you do to cope when things feel out of control?

PRAY

Dear God, thank you for being with me in a broken world. I know you have a wonderful home in store for me. Surround me with your peace and courage so that I can share your hope with others while I wait.

DO

It's not always easy to know when someone needs encouragement.

Be ready and on the lookout to share hope with others by coming up with a list of things you can do to make someone smile.

Make the Big Idea Personal

KNOW

Big Question: What am I doing here?

Big Idea: I was made on purpose, for a purpose.

Bible Verse: "For we are God's workmanship, created in Christ Jesus to do good works, which God prepared in advance for us to do." Ephesians 2:10 NIV

When God made you, he put you right where he wanted you and gave you gifts and abilities you can use to glorify him. God wants you to use what you have to love him and to help people join his family. That's his purpose for you.

Living out your purpose is hard, though. You might not feel smart, grown-up, pretty or cool enough.

Want to know the truth? God loves you just the way you are. He doesn't need you to be smart, grown-up, pretty or cool. He just needs you to say, "Yes, God, use me!"

God loves you very much; he won't make you do something you don't want to. He let's you decide if you want to fulfill his purpose. Whatever you choose, remember: your decision makes a difference.

THINK

Almost everyone worries about whether they're good enough or if a big sacrifice (like living for God) is worth it.

When you think about living for God's purpose, what worries or scares you?

PRAY

Jesus, I know you love me, and I want to love you, too. I worry about _____. Please give me peace. Help me trust you'll enable me to fulfill your purpose.

DO

Life with God is the best life you can have, on earth and in heaven.

Draw, write, or act out your favorite way to spend time with God.

Spending Time with God

Draw your favorite activities to do with God below.

Get to Know the Big Idea: Worship

The amazing textures, tastes, sights, smells and sounds around you are designed to make it so that you can't help but wonder who came up with all of these incredible ideas.

God wants you to know without a doubt that he exists and desires your friendship. A friendship with God begins with worship.

Worship is more than just singing; it's anything you do for God's pleasure, no matter where you are or who you're with. Worship is how you express love for God and show others you're part of his family.

KNOW

Big Question: What does God want from me?

Big Idea: I'm made to love God

Bible Verse: "Love the Lord your God with all your heart and with all your soul and with all your mind and with all your strength." Mark 12:30 NIV

Any time you obey God, you worship him. You show him he's more important than anything else (like popularity, money or your own comfort).

You're incredibly important to God and deeply loved by him. Knowing this and responding to it by loving him in return is the kind of grateful, heart-deep worship God wants most.

_____

_____

_____

_____

_____

_____

_____

_____

_____

_____

_____

_____

_____

_____

_____

_____

_____

THINK

You can worship even while doing chores by changing your attitude and inviting God to work with you.

1. Describe an attitude that doesn't please God and one that does.

2. What can help you change your attitude?

PRAY

You've got lots of love for me, Lord. I'm grateful that I'm so important to you. When I forget why I'm here or get frustrated with where I'm at in life, remind me that I was made to worship you.

DO

Learning what pleases God is the first step of worship. Doing what pleases him is the next.

Find out what pleases God by completing the activity on the next page.

Things That Please God

Look up the Bible verses below and fill in the missing words. Then draw a line to connect the words you found to their definition. Circle one Bible verse you can put into practice this week.

What does the Lord require of you? To act _____ and to love

_____ and to walk _____ with your God.

Definitions

To give something undeserved	Without thinking of my own importance	A manner that is honest and fair

And do not forget to do _____ and to _____

with others, for with such _____ God is pleased.

Definitions

The giving of something you care about	Something that benefits someone	To give what is yours to another

Without _____ it is impossible to please God . . . Anyone

who comes to him must _____ that he exists and that he

rewards those who earnestly _____ him.

Definitions

To desire and pursue more of something	To trust in something	A firm belief in something or someone

How to Make God Smile

It can be easy to think that a God as big as yours is hard to please. The thought of being around someone so powerful might even scare you. The Bible assures believers, though, that there's nothing to fear: there are countless ways to make God smile.

He smiles when you love him more than anyone and anything else. That means doing what God wants instead of what you or others want.

He smiles when you trust him no matter how you feel or what's happening around you. Sometimes this means waiting for a long time or not knowing all the answers.

Except for sinning, anything you do with appreciation and thankfulness brings a smile to God's face.

"Brothers and sisters, because of the great mercy God has shown us, offer your lives as a living sacrifice to him—an offering that is only for God and pleasing to him. Considering what he has done, it is only right that you should worship him in this way."

THINK

Keeping an attitude of appreciation helps you worship God no matter what you do.

Share about a time you worshipped God by doing something with the right attitude.

PRAY

Jesus, thank you for creating thousands of things just to make me smile. Teach me to notice and enjoy them. I want to make you smile, too, God. Change my attitude so I appreciate you, no matter what I'm going through.

DO

Even when things don't go the way you want them to, you can make God smile by trusting that he's still looking out for you.

Ask your grown-up to tell you about a time they trusted God even when things didn't look good.

DAY 10

Wholehearted Worship

People like flashy things: big houses, new clothes, nice hair and fancy toys. You might like flashy things so much you forget that God doesn't care about them––and he doesn't want them.

What could God want if he's not interested in his own tablet, brand new art supplies or the fastest bike?

God wants your *surrender*. That means you promise to obey what he says and trust that he'll take care of you, even when it doesn't make sense. Surrender is what turns *work* into *worship*. You willingly do what God asks instead of what you want because you believe he knows better than you do.

Jesus "watched the crowd putting their money into the offering boxes. Many rich people threw large amounts into them. But a poor widow came and put in two very small copper coins. They were worth only a few pennies."

Jesus said, "That poor widow has put more into the offering box than all the others . . . She gave even though she is poor. She put in everything she had."

28

NOTES

_____

_____

_____

_____

_____

_____

_____

_____

_____

_____

_____

_____

_____

_____

_____

_____

_____

_____

THINK

The widow gave all she had because she loved God more than money. She also trusted him to take care of her even if that meant giving him all the money she had left.

Think about the things you have. Which is your favorite? Imagine it's the very last item you have. What would make it hard to give it to God?

PRAY

Lord Jesus, remind me that flashy things don't replace true worship. What you want the most from me is surrender. Help me to do that every day.

DO

You may or may not know what it feels like to trust God so much you give him all the money you have.

Play the game on the next page to experience the different kinds of giving from today's reading.

Wholehearted Giving

Play this game with an adult and one or two other people if you can.

Supplies
___ Treats

Directions
1. Grab a bag of treats.

2. Announce that players can eat their treats after you take a treat offering. Everyone will give two treats, just like the widow did.

3. Give half the players four treats and the other half two treats.

4. Take the offering, reminding players that they're each giving 2 treats.

5. Once the offering is done, tell players they can eat their treats. At this point, you might have some upset players.
   - Say, "Everyone gave the same amount: 2 treats. That's fair. But it seems that some people are upset."
   - Ask, "What are you upset about?

6. Bring it back to the story of the widow. Emphasize how some people gave out of their wealth while the widow gave out of her poverty.
   - Ask, "What's the difference between giving out of your wealth and giving out of your poverty?"
   - Ask, "Which one is harder?"
   - Ask, "Why would the widow give everything she has to live on?"

7. Help players apply the lesson to their own lives.
   - Say, "True worship only happens when you surrender to God: when you love him more than your favorite things, do what he asks and trust he's going to give you everything you need. Let's remind each other to surrender to God."

DAY 11

Starting a Friendship with God

KNOW

Big Question: What does God want from me?

Big Idea: I'm made to love God

Bible Verse: "Love the Lord your God with all your heart and with all your soul. Love him with all your mind and with all your strength." Mark 12:30 NIRV

Passage: John 15:1–8 NIRV

Think about your best friend. When did you meet and how did you become friends?

Most often, friendships grow over months, maybe even years. They grow through connection: Time spent talking and doing things together. They're strengthened by going through good and bad experiences with one another.

Your friendship with God is no different: it takes time and energy. You have to learn about God just like you do your friends. Accepting God's friendship is part of loving and worshipping him. It shows God and others how serious you are about being part of his family.

"'I [Jesus] am the vine. You are the branches. If you remain joined to me, and I to you, you will bear a lot of fruit. You can't do anything without me . . . When you bear a lot of fruit, it brings glory to my Father. It shows that you are my disciples.'"

31

THINK

There are many things you can that take away from your time with God.

1. What's an activity you might want to do instead of talk to God?

2. Who are some people you might want to spend time with instead of God?

PRAY

Jesus, my friendship with you is my responsibility. If I don't choose to spend time with you, I won't. I want to be your friend. Help me make time for you each day.

DO

Friendship with God is easier said than done. It's easy to get carried away doing other things.

Talk with your grown-up about your schedule. Set aside 10 minutes each day to spend with God.

DAY 12

Making God Your Best Friend

How often do you talk to your best friend? Think about how much you look forward to seeing that friend, how much fun you have when you're together and how hard it can be to part ways.

God wants you to feel the same way about him; he wants to be your best friend (without the good-byes!). Jesus lived a life completely obedient to God and died on the cross for you to have that chance.

Because of his sacrifice, you can pray without ceasing: You can think about and talk to God all day long. You can invite him to be part of what you're doing (even if it's feeding the dog!). Whatever you're doing, remember: Your prayers don't have to be fancy. They only have to be honest.

Jesus says, "Here I am! I stand at the door and knock. If anyone hears my voice and opens the door, I will come in and eat with that person, and they with me."

THINK

Prayers can be simple, even when spoken to someone as important and powerful as God. The Holy Spirit helps your whole message (the parts you know how to say and the parts you don't) get through to God.

What can you say to God when you're:
- On the bus?
- At the store?
- Making your bed?
- Upset with your grown-up?

PRAY

Dear God, I'm so thankful I don't have to use fancy words for you to understand me. I'm also glad the Holy Spirit tells you what I'm going through when I can't. Teach me to pray without ceasing.

DO

The most important thing about prayer is that it's genuine: You say the words you want to say.

Complete the activity on the next page for an example of a simple prayer.

Simple Prayer Fill-in-the-Blank

The best prayers come from the heart. You can tell God exactly what you think, even if it's not nice (after all, he knows you're still learning to listen and obey him). There's nothing you can think, do or say to make him love you less.

Here's a simple prayer Jesus taught his followers to pray. It's called "The Lord's Prayer" and you can find it in Matthew 6:9–13 NLT. Fill in the blanks with a word from the word bank to complete the prayer.

Word Bank

temptation   food   kingdom   forgive
holy   earth   sin   will   heaven   rescue

"Pray like this:

'Our Father in _____ ,

    may your name be kept _____ .

May your _____ come soon.

May your _____ be done on _____ ,

    as it is in heaven.

Give us today the _____ we need,

    and _____ us our sins,

    as we have forgiven those who _____ against us.

And don't let us yield to _____ ,

    but _____ us from the evil one.'"

DAY 13

What God Wants Most

KNOW

Big Question: What does God want from me?

Big Idea: I'm made to love God

Bible Verse: "Love the Lord your God with all your heart and with all your soul. Love him with all your mind and with all your strength." Mark 12:30 NIRV

Passage: Acts 17:22–31 NIRV

Maybe one of the greatest blessings of friendship is having someone to talk to and do things with. Friends have a deeper understanding of what you're going through than most people. They know how to cheer you up, what kind of treats you like and where your favorite hiding spot is.

God wants his relationship with you to reflect your friendships. He wants to know what you dream of becoming, how your day went and why you're upset with yourself.

God is older than dinosaurs. He knows more than the internet. He made the dirt stuck to your shoes! And he wants to be a part of your life. He wants to comfort you when you cry, guide you when you're lost and be right by your side when it's time to be brave.

"God did this so that people would seek him. And perhaps they would reach out for him and find him. They would find him even though he is not far from any of us."

NOTES

THINK

Becoming best friends with God is something that will take the rest of your life. It takes learning to worship God through loving, trusting, obeying and serving him.

What are some things you can do to spend time with God?

PRAY

Father God, learning to live a life of worship is going to take a lifetime. I'm thankful I have my church family to support me. Show me how to be a good friend to them and to you.

DO

Having a relationship with someone you can't see or touch can be tricky. Where do you start?

Ask your grown-up how they experience God. How do they build their relationship with him?

DAY 14

Make the Big Idea Personal

This is worship: your love, trust, obedience and service to something or someone. God, the creator of the entire universe, wants your worship. Not your iPad or new shoes. He wants your friendship: your time, attention and dedication.

God loves you so much. He wants you to have a great life. He also knows he's the only one who can take perfect care of you. Being your friend gives him the chance to do both those things.

But here's the catch: He's not going to make you listen or obey him. That's not what friends do! He wants you to say, "Yes, God, I want to be your friend. You're in charge."

KNOW

Big Question: What does God want from me?

Big Idea: I'm made to love God

Bible Verse: "Love the Lord your God with all your heart and with all your soul. Love him with all your mind and with all your strength." Mark 12:30 NIRV

When you're ready to start a friendship with God, tell your grown-up. They can pray with you and connect you with others who can help you grow closer to God.

38

_____

_____

_____

_____

_____

_____

_____

_____

_____

_____

_____

_____

_____

_____

_____

_____

_____

THINK

God wants to be your friend, but he loves you too much to make you do anything. Instead, he's given you the freedom to choose to be in a relationship with him.

1. Why would God let you decide if you're going to be his friend or not?

2. Do you want to be God's friend?

3. Ask your grown-up to share some pros and cons of being God's friend.

PRAY

Jesus, proof that you love me and want to be part of my life is all around me. Teach me how to be a true friend. Help me love you by worshipping you with my thoughts, words and actions.

DO

Worship is the thoughts you have, the words you say and actions you do that please God.

Think of all the different ways you can worship God. Do one you haven't done in a while.

Where do I belong?

PART 3: FELLOWSHIP

I'm made for God's family

DAY 15

Get to Know the Big Idea: Fellowship

KNOW

Big Question: Where do I belong?

Big Idea: I'm made for God's family

Bible Verse: "So in Christ we, though many, form one body, and each member belongs to all the others." Romans 12:5 NIV

Your world and all the galaxies around it are old. Older than your grown-up, older than your house and older than the oldest grandparent you've ever seen!

You may live in an ancient universe, but God's hope for you has always been the same: that you do life in community. This means you belong with a group of people (made up of family, friends and neighbors) who celebrate good times and go through bad times with you.

But . . . where do you belong? The world is big and there are billions of people—how do you find people you like who like you back?

That's a good question, one the Bible talks about a lot. You were especially made for God's family. This is the group of people who love God; serve him with their thoughts, words and actions; invite others to be part of his family and show them how to live for God. This is the group of people who make a promise to become like Christ and fulfill that promise together. This is where you are made to belong.

THINK

Think about your family. There might be people who love God and people who don't know him yet.

1. What's helpful about being part of God's family?

2. How can you show God's love to those who don't know him yet?

PRAY

Thanks for giving me a place in your family, God. There are lots of people who can teach me how to love you and others. There are also lots of people who need to experience your love. Humble me so that I learn. Make me bold me so that I share your love.

DO

Whether you know it or not, God can use what you say and do to influence the people around you.

Who's affected by your words and actions? Pray for your influence to be a blessing.

NOTES

_____
_____
_____
_____
_____
_____
_____
_____
_____
_____
_____
_____
_____
_____
_____
_____
_____
_____
_____
_____

Who's Who in God's Family?

Mommy, daddy, auntie, uncle, grandma, grandpa, cousin. People have different titles depending on how they're related to you.

God's family is a little different. In his family, everyone is his *child* and he's their *Father*. That means you're his child—and so is your grown-up! It might be a little weird to think about it that way, but there's a good reason why there's only one Father in God's family.

God takes care of us, leads us and disciplines us just like an earthly father would. The big difference is that he does it *perfectly*. As much as your grown-up loves you, sometimes they miss the mark. They don't always respond to you the way you need them to.

KNOW

Big Question: Where do I belong?

Big Idea: I'm made for God's family.

Bible Verse: "So in Christ we, though many, form one body, and each member belongs to all the others." Romans 12:5 NIV

Passage: 1 John 3:1-2 NIRV

God's different. In every situation, he knows how to talk to, correct, heal and comfort you exactly the way you need it. He's a 100% good father to his children.

"See what amazing love the Father has given us! Because of it, we are called children of God. And that's what we really are!"

45

_____

_____

_____

_____

_____

_____

_____

_____

_____

_____

_____

_____

_____

_____

_____

_____

_____

_____

THINK

Many earthly fathers are loving--but not all are. God knows this. It breaks his heart when his children get hurt. He wants to show everyone what a good father is like.

1. What are things a loving father does and says?

3. How does a loving father make you feel?

PRAY

Lord Jesus, being a part of your family is a blessing. Thank you for thinking of me! Remind me that you're always on my side, no matter how I feel. My soul blesses you, Lord.

DO

As your father, God knows what's best for you. What he wants most will help you live the best life you can on earth.

Complete the puzzle on the next page to find out how to do that.

46

What God Wants Most

Solve the puzzle then draw a picture of what God wants most.

```
A   B   C   D   E   F   G   H   I   J   K   L   M
1   2   3   4   5   6   7   8   9   10  11  12  13

N   O   P   Q   R   S   T   U   V   W   X   Y   Z
14  15  16  17  18  19  20  21  22  23  24  25  26
```

"I don't want your ___ ___ ___ ___ ___ ___ ___ ___ ___ ___
                       19 1 3 18 9 6 9 3 5 19

I want your ___ ___ ___ ___;
              12 15 22 5

I don't want your ___ ___ ___ ___ ___ ___ ___ ___
               15 6 6 5 18 9 14 7 19

I want you to ___ ___ ___ ___ me."
          11 14 15 23

Hosea 6:6 TLB

DAY 17

Love Makes a Family

KNOW

Big Question: Where do I belong?

Big Idea: I'm made for God's family

Bible Verse: "So in Christ we, though many, form one body, and each member belongs to all the others." Romans 12:5 NIV

Passage: Acts 2:42–47 NIRV

Think about all the things that fill the world: people, bugs, rocks, books, toys, cars and electronics. The list is endless! Of all the things that God's made, what do you think matters the most to him?

That's a tricky question! What matters most to God isn't something you can see. It also looks different from person to person. But it's always marked by the same quality: love.

What matters most to God is that you love him. How do you show him you love him? By loving the people he's created. Love others the same way you love God: with your thoughts, words and actions.

"The believers studied what the apostles taught. They shared their lives together. They ate and prayed together . . . They shared everything they had. They sold property and other things they owned. They gave to anyone who needed something. Every day they met together in the temple courtyard. They ate meals together in their homes. Their hearts were glad and sincere."

THINK

Relationships give you a chance to love others and to be loved by others.

1. Who are some of your favorite people?

2. What are some things they do that make you feel loved?

3. How do you show love to others?

PRAY

Dear God, thank you for the people I have in my life. I'm grateful they love me, teach me and look out for me. When I forget to love others with my thoughts, words and actions, remind me that love matters most.

DO

Since the day you were born, you've given and received love. What's more amazing is that there's more than one way to love.

Figure out your love language on the next page.

NOTES

_____

_____

_____

_____

_____

_____

_____

_____

_____

_____

_____

_____

_____

_____

_____

_____

_____

_____

_____

Love Languages

A smart guy named Gary Chapman did research and discovered that there are at least 5 different ways people give and receive love. Sometimes, the language you speak is different from the one you like to receive. For example, you might be really good at giving hugs but like it most when someone gives you gifts.

Learning the love language you speak can help you teach others how to love you and show you how to love others better.

Which language do you speak and which do you give? Circle 1 or 2 of the pictures below that show the love language you speak most.

Teamwork Wins

How many parts does your body have? Too many to count! Think about how God gave all of those parts their own special job and designed them to work together to help you live your life. Each one is important for you to function.

Being part of God's family is like being part of a body: You work with others towards the same goal. In this case, it's showing and telling people about God. You're incredibly important because of the gifts, skills and abilities you have. At the same time, you're made to work best when you work with others.

KNOW

Big Question: Where do I belong?

Big Idea: I'm made for God's family

Bible Verse: "So in Christ we, though many, form one body, and each member belongs to all the others." Romans 12:5 NIV

Passage: 1 Corinthians 12:12-27 NIRV

"There is one body, but it has many parts. But all its many parts make up one body. It is the same with Christ. We were all baptized by one Holy Spirit. And so we are formed into one body . . . So the body is not made up of just one part. It has many parts . . . God has placed each part in the body just as he wanted it to be."

As you experience life with others, you grow. You learn how to be an honest, sympathetic and merciful team player.

NOTES

_____

_____

_____

_____

_____

_____

_____

_____

_____

_____

_____

_____

_____

_____

_____

_____

_____

THINK

Life is meant to be shared; you're made to be part of a team. Great things can come from teamwork, but it sure isn't easy.

1. What's great about being part of a team?

2. What's hard about being part of a team?

PRAY

Thanks for giving me the chance to be part of your family, Jesus. It's not always easy when I'm part of a team, but it helps me become more like you. Give me courage to grow.

DO

Even though there will be times when you don't get along with (or even like) family members, disputes can help you grow.

Think of someone you recently upset. Make a list of how you can apologize to them and then make amends.

Building a Strong Family

KNOW

Big Question: Where do I belong?

Big Idea: I'm made for God's family

Bible Verse: "So in Christ we, though many, form one body, and each member belongs to all the others." Romans 12:5 NIV

Passage: Ephesians 4:2-6, NIRV

Families help each other, but not all help feels good. Sometimes you grow the most when you're in uncomfortable situations: times when you upset, disagree with, need to reconcile with or ask for forgiveness from those you care about. Healthy families go through hard times *and* get through them together.

Building a strong family is hard and often intimidating work. It's a promise to tell the truth, to understand you're not always right, to respect differences and to look out for your family members––even if it means saying no to your own desires.

"Don't be proud at all. Be completely gentle. Be patient. Put up with one another in love. The Holy Spirit makes you one in every way. So try your best to remain as one. Let peace keep you together. There is one body and one Spirit . . . There is one Lord, one faith and one baptism. There is one God and Father of all. He is over everything. He is through everything. He is in everything."

THINK

Reminding others and being reminded yourself of what's right in God's eyes is part of building a strong family.

1. Why should you remind others to obey God?

2. What is humility? Why is it needed to build a strong family?

PRAY

Jesus, your life on earth showed me how to love my family. Love is kind, but it doesn't let others get away with sin. Teach me how to love like that and receive that love in return.

DO

Not very many people like to be corrected. It can be embarrassing. Still, God wants people in his family to remind one other to do what's right in his eyes.

Come up with a phrase you and your family can use to gently correct each other when tempers flare.

NOTES

_____
_____
_____
_____
_____
_____
_____
_____
_____
_____
_____
_____
_____
_____
_____
_____
_____
_____
_____
_____

DAY 20

Making Peace After Pain

All of God's people are part of the same body; you're on one team. But it doesn't always feel that way. It can feel as though you're in competition with each other. It can feel as though you're not good enough, as if you don't belong.

No family is perfect--God's family included. It's made up of sinful people in the *process* of being healed, but not healed yet. That leaves room for all sorts of brokenness: disagreements, harsh words, trauma and shame.

Try as anyone might to do what's right in God's eyes, there will be times sin wins. You do something that hurts someone. Or someone does something that hurts you. When this happens, find comfort knowing that God doesn't expect you to be perfect. He does, however, want you to make peace by seeking forgiveness and trying to make things right. You can do this by being honest, sympathetic, humble and committed to helping each other become more like Jesus.

"Get rid of all hard feelings, anger and rage. Stop all fighting and lying. Don't have anything to do with any kind of hatred. Be kind and tender to one another. Forgive one another, just as God forgave you because of what Christ has done."

_____

_____

_____

_____

_____

_____

_____

_____

_____

_____

_____

_____

_____

_____

_____

_____

THINK

At times you'll know when you hurt someone and at other times, you won't even notice.

1. Is there anyone you may have upset recently?

2. What can you do to make amends?

PRAY

God, pour your power, healing, and peace over me today. Hug me and let me know you're here. Give me courage to seek peace and make things right with those I've wronged.

DO

Making peace after pain means looking for ways to start the healing process after a relationship has been broken.

Flip to the next page to learn about different ways to make amends.

Apology Languages

"Making amends" is another way to say "making things right." When you have to make amends, it's usually with a person you disagreed with. The tension you were experiencing may have led you to say or do things that hurt them--and they might have hurt you, too.

When people in a relationship cause each other pain, the best way to make peace after the pain is to make amends: Each person has to make things right with the other individual. This includes asking for forgiveness and then showing with your actions that you're committed to doing better next time.

Because everyone is unique, how you make amends will be different from one person to the next. Gary Chapman, the same guy who came up with the love languages, discovered that there are also *apology languages*, or common ways in which people say they're sorry (told you he's smart!).

Read through the apology languages below. Which do you use and which do you respond to best?

Now consider this: Which language works best with the people you care about? The answer to that one will likely be different for each person. Part of making amends to the best of your ability is learning to apologize in the way others respond to best. It's hard work, but a sure sign that you're committed to loving someone well.

To help you remember how to apologize to the important people in your life, take notes using the chart at the end of the activity.

EXPRESSING REGRET

You can tell if someone means what they say, and you take it seriously. When someone says, "I'm sorry," from the bottom of their heart, you know it. That's exactly what you need to make amends.

ACCEPTING RESPONSIBILITY

It's important to you that someone knows what they did wrong and apologizes for how they hurt you. When someone wants to make amends, part of it needs to include something along the lines of, "I'm sorry. I was wrong about _____."

Apology Languages (cont.)

GENUINELY REPENTING

Hearing an apology is important to you, but so is knowing what the person who hurt you will do next time to avoid hurting you again. Making amends may sound like, "I'm sorry. Next time, I'll _____ instead."

MAKING RESTITUTION

This apology language centers around actions: You'll know someone is sorry because of what they do. An apology you'll appreciate will sound like, "I'm sorry. What can I do to make it up to you?" with the person doing what you said thereafter.

REQUESTING FORGIVENESS

You may be someone who needs to hear, "Will you please forgive me?" as a part of making amends. If this is you, do your best to give yourself space so you can decide if and when you're ready to forgive the person who hurt you.

Person	Apology Language
1.	
2.	
3.	
4.	
5.	

Make the Big Idea Personal

KNOW

Big Question: Where do I belong?

Big Idea: I'm made for God's family

Bible Verse: "So in Christ we, though many, form one body, and each member belongs to all the others." Romans 12:5 NIV

Just as it is with any other family, being part of God's family has its pros and cons. Pros include having guidance from people who love you and God. These same people also experience life with you. They keep you on a path that glorifies God, which involves both supporting and correcting you.

Cons include saying yes to growing in hard ways: admitting you don't always know or do what's right, changing bad habits, and learning new ones. It also means helping others do the same (which isn't always enjoyable or easy).

You might be deserted, teased or rejected by those who don't care for God, including people you love. You may have to distance yourself from them. You might have to stop doing things you enjoy because they don't honor God.

Saying yes to joining his family might mean saying no to people or things you care about. Thankfully, you have "siblings" in God's family who are going through similar situations and understand what you're going through. In God's family, you're never alone!

THINK

Saying no to people and things you care about is hard.

1. How can you say "no" to someone who wants you to do something that would hurt God or others?

2. What are some things you might have to say no to?

PRAY

Until you come back for me, Lord Jesus, there will always be pros and cons to being part of your family. When it gets hard to obey you, remind me to ask for help. When I don't obey, remind me to ask for forgiveness and guidance.

DO

It can be easy to forget that there are people who love God and love you (especially when you feel discouraged or defeated).

Complete "My Church Family" on the next page to see who can help when you're in need.

NOTES

My Church Family

God's family is spread across the world. There are people in hundreds of countries telling others about God's love and inviting them to join his family. Your church family is part of God's family. They're people whom you see and grow with on a regular basis, at church and within the community.

Draw or glue a picture of some of your favorite people in your church family. Then answer the questions. You can add more family members on the next page.

_____ is important

to me because _____

_____

_____.

_____ is important

to me because _____

_____

_____.

_____ is important

to me because _____

_____

_____.

_____ is important

to me because _____

_____

_____.

God's family looks like _____.

God's family feels like _____.

My Church Family (cont.)

_____ is important

to me because _____

_____

_____.

_____ is important

to me because _____

_____

_____.

_____ is important

to me because _____

_____

_____.

_____ is important

to me because _____

_____

_____.

_____ is important

to me because _____

_____

_____.

_____ is important

to me because _____

_____

_____.

What kind of person do I want to be?

PART 4: DISCIPLESHIP

I'm made to become Like Jesus

Get to Know the Big Idea: Discipleship

When God made you, he made you in his image. That means you look like him on the outside and *inside*. You can laugh like God, relax like God, and feel upset like God––all without trying. But to *be* like God? Now that takes effort.

God sent Jesus to show you what he looks like on the inside: what he cares about, how to love him and how to treat others. When you do what Jesus does with the same attitude he has, you become more Christ–like (Christ is another name Jesus had).

KNOW

Big Question: What kind of person do I want to be?

Big Idea: I'm made to become like Jesus

Bible Verse: "Your attitude should be the same as that of Christ Jesus." Philippians 2:5 NIV

Becoming Christ–like is a journey full of unknowns, dead ends and plot twists. This journey is called "discipleship," and God's calling you to this adventure.

He loves you just the way you are. He knows, though, that the best life you can have on earth is one where you're most like Jesus: connected to your heavenly Father and strengthened by his always–present, never–tired, greater–than–everything power.

65

You often do what the people around you do. God wants you to be so close to him that you do what he does, too.

1. Name something you do that a grown-up in your life does.

2. Name something you do that God does.

PRAY

I become most like the people I surround myself with. Lord God, I want to be like you. Teach me more about you and help me live a life of worship that pleases you.

DO

Everyone has habits that don't please God, even people in God's family. To be Christ-like, trade these habits for ones that glorify God.

Tell your grown up one bad habit you have and ask them to share one.

DAY 23

Time to Grow!

Sometimes you grow without having to think about it--like how your hair and legs get long all on their own. Other times, you have to tell yourself it's time to grow--like when you want to be more Christ-like.

God's goal for everyone in his family is Christ-likeness: Thinking, speaking, and acting like Jesus with the same God-pleasing attitude. But he won't make you do it. He gives you the freedom to choose if you want to be Christ-like.

When you join God's family, you make a promise to live like Jesus. That's a hard job, though. God knows this. That's why he sends the Holy Spirit to help you get there. Each time you're faced with the chance to do what's right in God's eyes or sin, the Holy Spirit reminds you to choose God's way.

"The Spirit gives love, joy, peace, patience, kindness, goodness, faithfulness, gentleness, self-control. There is no law that says these things are wrong."

THINK

Discipleship is a hard, life-long process. You'll need people to help you stay on track. This is known as *accountability*.

1. Who can keep you accountable on your discipleship journey?

2. What can they do to help?

PRAY

Dear God, making any kind of commitment can be scary. Committing to become Christ-like is worth it, though. Remind me of the things you care about so that I can glorify you with my thoughts, words and actions.

DO

It can be easy to forget that you made a promise to become Christ-like. Printables can help you remember.

Color in and cut out "Christ-like Printables" in Appendix A.

DAY 24

Changed by the Truth

One time, Jesus' parents lost track of him (true story!). They found him at the temple, teaching people about things he had learned from the Bible. People were amazed: Jesus was young but had a deep understanding of God's words.

Understanding what the Bible says is a big part of discipleship. God uses the Bible to show you what he's like, his plan to heal all brokenness and how his family contributes to that plan. It's always true no matter how you feel, what goes on in the world or what others say.

With the Holy Spirit's help, the Bible can change your life with its truth. Believe it, meditate on it and do what it says. Soak up God's words like a sponge so that Christ-likeness can ooze out of you.

"All Scripture is inspired by God and is useful to teach us what is true and to make us realize what is wrong in our lives. It corrects us when we are wrong and teaches us to do what is right. God uses it to prepare and equip his people to do every good work."

NOTES

_____

_____

_____

_____

_____

_____

_____

_____

_____

_____

_____

_____

_____

_____

_____

_____

THINK

Reading the Bible isn't enough to be changed by it. You've got to reflect on it, too. When you read, ask yourself these questions:

1. What is the writer saying?
2. How do I live by this truth?

PRAY

Dear God, I want to be more like Jesus, but I need your help! Remind me to read my Bible, reflect on what I learn and do what it says.

DO

People learn in all sorts of ways. Bible makers know this and have created a variety of Bibles in hopes that God's message reaches everyone.

Read about different learning styles and Bibles on the next pages.

Different Learning Styles

God has created over 7 billion people who look, think and experience the world in different ways. He's so creative that he's even made it possible for us to learn differently, too. Look over the learning styles below. Which one describes you? It's likely many of them overlap for you, making it easy to say you learn through most, if not all, of the styles. For this activity, just pick one or two that describe your favorite way to learn. Understanding how you learn can help you find a Bible that you'll enjoy reading every day.

Visual Learners
You learn best when you see what you're learning. You like information presented to you in pictures, graphs, charts or videos. You might learn better when you can doodle or color while you listen.

Auditory Learners
You learn best when you hear what you're learning. It might even be best if you're *only* listening, without other distractions. You like information presented to you with spoken word, music or sound.

Verbal Learners
You learn best when you can use words to process what you're learning. You like to talk about information, whether out loud or on paper. The more you talk, the better you're able to understand the information you were given.

Kinesthetic Learners
You learn best when your body is engaged in the process. You like to move as you learn, whether that's tinkering with objects, fiddling with a pencil or toy as you listen or going for a walk so you can think.

Different Learning Styles (cont.)

Logical Learners

You learn best when content makes sense (and if it doesn't, you might get upset). You process information like you would a puzzle: each piece has a place and all parts need to fit together. You like information presented to you with facts, numbers and systems.

Naturalist Learners

You learn best when you can be around or interact with nature. You like to gather information hands on by interacting with or observing things found in nature. Sometimes, simply being outside of a building gives you enough brain power to learn at your best.

Social Learners

You learn best when you learn with someone else. Processing information or coming up with new ideas alongside others motivates and energizes you.

Solitary Learners

You learn best on your own. Your optimal learning space gives you the chance to find, work through and make sense of information by yourself.

Bibles for All Learners

Since there are a variety of learning styles, it only makes sense that there are a variety of Bibles, too. There are almost 700 different translations of the Bible—that 700 different ways to share God's truth! Each translation gives a unique group of people the chance to hear, understand and say yes to being part of God's story.

Now that you know a little more about how you learn best, take a look at some of the unique Bibles available. Is there one that you'd look forward to reading each day? If so, talk with your adult about saving up to get it.

THE ACTION BIBLE

By Doug Mauss and Sergio Cariello

Journey through 215 stories of the Bible from start to finish—comic book style! The Action Bible is beautifully illustrated and keeps you on the edge of your seat.

THE ADVENTURE BIBLE

By Zondervan

Explore Scripture with a jungle-themed Bible. It comes packed with colorful illustrations, practical applications, biographies, and historical facts about Bible times.

INTERNATIONAL CHILDREN'S BIBLE

By Thomas Nelson

Instill "quiet time" early on with this written-for-kids translation. It offers larger type, a dictionary, a concordance and over 300 verses highlighted for memorization.

THE JESUS STORYBOOK BIBLE

By Sally Lloyd Jones and Jago

Discover how stories of the Bible point to Jesus' purpose and sacrifice. The culturally-accurate illustrations beautifully depict how God revealed his great plan for his people from the Old Testament to the New.

Bibles for All Learners (cont.)

THE WAYFINDING BIBLE

By Tyndale

Approach reading the Word through one of three routes: Flyover, Direct or Scenic. Stops, historical markers, side trips and scenic overlooks await in this choose-your-adventure styled Bible.

THE HANDS-ON BIBLE

By Tyndale

Soak in God's Word through your senses! This Bible is packed with crafts, experiments and tasty activities to engage your eyes, ears, taste buds, nose and hands. Make learning the Word a memorable experience!

THE BEGINNER'S BIBLE AUDIO

By Zondervan

Listen along to more than 90 Bible stories from both the Old and New Testaments. This audio collection is great for young kids who prefer auditory learning or for caregivers who are looking for a way to change up Bible study with a listening-only challenge.

LAUGH AND GROW BIBLE

By Phil Vischer

Tackle Bible reading for the whole family (in five minutes!) In a fun-filled setting that helps grown-ups and kids learn about, reflect on and live out the big picture behind God's story.

These are only a few of the countless Bibles there are. They've been designed to help all sorts of learners access the most important thing there is to learn about: God! Circle three that sound most interesting. Consider asking for them on birthdays, holidays or from your church as a tool to help you grow spiritually.

Changed By Trouble

Do you like having troubles? Chances are you're like most people and prefer it when things go the way they're supposed to go. Troubles are hard and inconvenient. Sometimes, they even make you cry.

God doesn't like to see you struggle, work until you're exhausted or cry. But he does like seeing you become Christ-like. He knows a Christ-like life is the most satisfying life you can have on earth; so if you let him, he uses trouble to transform you.

Having troubles will never be fun, but you can experience peace even in the middle of them when you know that God is on your side, using those troubles for his good plan.

"Our troubles are small. They last only for a short time. But they are earning for us a glory that will last forever. It is greater than all our troubles. So we don't spend all our time looking at what we can see. Instead, we look at what we can't see . . . . What can't be seen will last forever."

THINK

Sometimes you know what God's doing and sometimes you don't. In the end, God works to glorify himself and make you more like Jesus.

Think of a trouble you're having. How might God use it to transform you?

PRAY

Lord Jesus, things won't always go my way. When I'm having troubles, please remind me that you're in control and love me no matter what happens. Wrap me in your peace so I can trust you while I wait.

DO

Troubles can be so painful that people get stuck in the negative feelings and habits they bring. Transformation that lasts only comes when you let God heal your heart.

Ask your grown-up to tell you about a trouble God used to transform them.

NOTES

_____

_____

_____

_____

_____

_____

_____

_____

_____

_____

_____

_____

_____

_____

_____

_____

_____

_____

DAY 26

Changed Through Temptation

Doing the right thing isn't always easy. Sometimes you'll want to sin because it's easier or more fun. Whenever you think about doing things you know you shouldn't do (because it could hurt you, others or God) you experience *temptation*.

Everyone is tempted, including Jesus when he was on earth. Temptation itself isn't bad; it's a part of discipleship. It's the choice you make when you're tempted that either glorifies God or doesn't.

Whenever you have the chance to sin, you also have the chance to do what's right in God's eyes. When you do what's right instead of sinning, you honor God by thinking, speaking and acting as Jesus would.

KNOW

Big Question: What kind of person do I want to be?

Big Idea: I'm made to become like Jesus

Bible Verse: "Your attitude should be the same as that of Christ Jesus." Philippians 2:5 NIV

Passage: 1 Corinthians 10:13 NIRV

"You are tempted in the same way all other human beings are. God is faithful. He will not let you be tempted any more than you can take. But when you are tempted, God will give you a way out. Then you will be able to deal with it."

77

NOTES

_____

_____

_____

_____

_____

_____

_____

_____

_____

_____

_____

_____

_____

_____

_____

_____

_____

THINK

Unfortunately, temptation is not something you outgrow. You'll face it every day for the rest of your life. Thankfully, you'll have God and your church family to help you through it.

What's something you're tempted by on most days?

PRAY

Lord, facing temptation can be intimidating. Teach me how to win over sin. When I fail to do what's right, remind me that you're still on my side, ready to help the next time temptation comes around.

DO

You can be ready to overcome temptation by learning to recognize it.

Think through what temptation looks like for you by completing the activity on the next page.

Recognizing Temptation

Temptations are thoughts you have about doing things that would hurt God, yourself or others. These thoughts suggest you say or do things that go against what God wants. Temptations are not sin; they are a *desire* to sin. If you do what's right in God's eyes, you overcome temptation. If you don't, you give in to temptation and sin.

The Bible urges you to fight the devil when he comes around to tempt you. Don't listen to what he says! "Obey God. Stand up to the devil. He will run away from you" (James 4:7 NIRV).

Fighting the devil looks different for everyone. What stays the same is the desire to do what's right in God's eyes. The more you know about your temptations, the better you can avoid or overcome them.

Temptations might be easy to overlook (like yelling at your siblings when they touch your things) or hard to miss (like breaking the rules on purpose). List some of the temptations you face most days. Circle whether it's related to a person, place or thing. Then think over the last week and estimate the number of days you faced that temptation.

1. _____

_____

This temptation is about a: person   place   thing

The times I faced this temptation each week (circle):

Sunday   Monday   Tuesday   Wednesday   Thursday   Friday   Saturday

morning   afternoon   evening   night

When faced with this temptation, I feel (circle):

powerless   forgotten   unloved   unsafe   other: _____

What I think will help me overcome this temptation:

a friend   a distraction   a change of scenery   other: _____

79

2. _____

_____

This temptation is about a: person   place   thing

The times I faced this temptation each week (circle):

Sunday   Monday   Tuesday   Wednesday   Thursday   Friday   Saturday

morning   afternoon   evening   night

When faced with this temptation, I feel (circle):

powerless   forgotten   unloved   unsafe   other: _____

What I think will help me overcome this temptation:

a friend   a distraction   a change of scenery   other: _____

3. _____

_____

This temptation is about a: person   place   thing

The times I faced this temptation each week (circle):

Sunday   Monday   Tuesday   Wednesday   Thursday   Friday   Saturday

morning   afternoon   evening   night

When faced with this temptation, I feel (circle):

powerless   forgotten   unloved   unsafe   other: _____

Recognizing Temptation (cont.)

What I think will help me overcome this temptation:

a friend   a distraction   a change of scenery   other: _____

If there's a certain person, place or thing that you're tempted with more often than others, make note of it here:

It seems like _____ is a big source

of temptation in my life.

If there's a certain day of the week or time of the day that you feel especially tempted, make note of it here:

I feel especially tempted on/during: _____

If there's a certain person or tool that you think can help you overcome the temptations you face, make note of it here:

_____ can help me overcome temptation

Look over the temptations you listed. Which one do you experience most?

A big temptation I have right now is _____

_____

Great work! You've done some important reflection on temptation. Tomorrow you'll use this activity to create a plan to overcome temptation.

Overcoming Temptation

KNOW

Big Question: What kind of person do I want to be?

Big Idea: I'm made to become like Jesus

Bible Verse: "Your attitude should be the same as that of Christ Jesus." Philippians 2:5 NIV

Passage: Philippians 4:13 NIRV

Name something you're really good at. How did you get good at it?

Learning to do something well takes a lot of time, energy and sometimes even resources. Learning to overcome temptation each time you face it is the same: It's going to take some hard work. You'll mess up, especially in the beginning. But the longer you stick with it, the better you'll get at defeating temptation.

God knows fighting the devil and becoming Christ-like is hard--so hard it's going to take your *entire* life to learn! He's sent the Holy Spirit to guide you every step of the way. The Holy Spirit is God's helper. Part of his job includes reminding you of what's right in God's eyes and helping you do it. He'll always step in when you ask for his help. Whenever you feel the desire to sin, the Holy Spirit is ready to help you say, "No!"

"I can do all this by the power of Christ. He gives me strength."

THINK

Sometimes, you might feel like giving up because it seems as though the battle to do what's right never ends.

What's something you can say or do to celebrate the times you overcome temptation?

PRAY

Dear God, thank you that I don't have to fight temptation on my own. Help me notice when I'm tempted. Remind me to do what's right. Show me the way out.

DO

Defeating temptation doesn't happen on its own. You've got to plan to overcome it and carry out the plan every time temptation strikes.

Using the activity on the next page, work with your grown-up to create a plan to win over sin.

Overcoming Temptation

Flip back to the activity you completed yesterday. Look for where you wrote down the biggest temptation you face right now. Copy it here:

_____

_____

Since you face this temptation the most at the moment, you're going to create a plan to overcome this one first. If you like this process, you can repeat the next steps with the other temptations.

When you're ready, answer the following questions:

1. Is this temptation about a person, place or thing?

2. Is there a way you can avoid this person, place or thing? If so, write it

down: _____

_____

3. If not, is there a way you can have someone or something with you to remind you to overcome the temptation when you're around it? If so, write down the name of that someone or something:

_____

_____

4. If not, brainstorm ways you can stay strong, fight the devil and win over sin when faced with this temptation. Use ideas on the next page or come up with your own.

– I can _____

– I can _____

– I can _____

Overcoming Temptation (cont.)

Ways to Win Over Sin

Recite a Bible verse

Go for a walk

Say a prayer

Find someone to help me

Take 5 deep breaths

Push against a wall as hard as I can

Blow 7 raspberries

Scream into a pillow

Hold my breath for as long as I can

Close my eyes and suck on candy

Give myself a tight hug

Ask someone to pray for me

Tighten my fists. Release.

Count my heartbeats

Leave the area

Sing a song

You did it! You've created a plan to overcome temptation. Now it's time for the hard part: sticking to your plan. Here are some steps to simplify this process:

1. Talk with your grown-up about when you're most likely to come face-to-face with this temptation.
2. Run through your plan, starting with how you'll avoid the temptation and ending with what you'll do to win over sin.
3. If needed, ask your grown-up to help you contact the person(s) or get the resource(s) that can help you overcome temptation.
4. If it helps, make copies of your plan and hang them up around the house so you can see and be reminded of how to win over sin.
5. Finally, ask your grown-up to help you remember your plan when temptation strikes.

Make the Big Idea Personal

You don't get to choose how tall you are, what color your skin is or who's a part of your family. But you do get to choose the kind of person you want to be. That's an important decision!

God sent Jesus to live, die and rise from the dead to show you the kind of person he is--and the kind of person he wants you to be, too. He made you to become like Jesus. He's given you the Holy Spirit and the Bible to guide you on the long and hard journey of discipleship. Jesus' sacrifice gives you the tools to face troubles and temptations with confidence that you can do what's right in God's eyes.

KNOW

Big Question: What kind of person do I want to be?

Big Idea: I'm made to become like Jesus

Bible Verse: "Your attitude should be the same as that of Christ Jesus." Philippians 2:5 NIV

Your best life on earth comes when you surrender to God's design. After all, he's the one who created you and knows you better than anyone (including yourself!). In this case, surrender means saying, "Yes, God. Make me Christ-like." His heart jumps with joy and he starts this good work at the sound of those words!

_____

_____

_____

_____

_____

_____

_____

_____

_____

_____

_____

_____

_____

_____

_____

_____

THINK

Discipleship is a journey to become like Christ: to think like him, speak like him and act like him.

Talk with your grown-up: Why do you think God says this is the best way to live life on earth?

PRAY

I'm made to become like you, Jesus. My life on earth is most satisfying when I follow your lead. Help me surrender to the Holy Spirit so he can make me more like you.

DO

There's no way to know you're growing unless you keep track of it.

Use the spiritual growth tracker on the next page to record where you are today. Then check back in 6 months or 1 year to see how much you've grown!

Spiritual Growth Tracker

All kinds of people followed Jesus: the curious and the committed. While he loves every single one of them, only those who are part of his family get to live with him forever.

Jesus wants his family to be healthy and close-knit. Becoming that kind of family takes work. Everyone has to do their part to keep the family healthy.

Keeping track of your spiritual growth is one way to do that. It shows you where you started your discipleship journey, where you are currently and where you want to go. By keeping track of how you grow, you can stay on track to keep growing!

Circle the description that best describes where you are today:

Stage	Jesus' Challenge	My Response	How I Grow	How I Become Christ-like
The Curious	"Come and see." Jn. 1:45–46	"I see."	Casual events	My thoughts are challenged
The Crowd	"Come learn from me." Mk. 10:1	"I hear."	Outreach events	My thoughts change
The Church-Goer	"Come follow me." Mat. 4:19	"I believe."	Church services	My habits change
The Committed	"Abide in me." 1 Jn. 2:24	"I press on."	Small group	My values change
The Core	"Serve me." 1 Pet. 4:10	"I serve."	Regular volunteerism, leadership	My gifts and skills bless others
The Commissioned	"Represent me" Mat. 28:18–20	"I go."	Leadership, missions	My life is God's to control

Inspired by Highland Park Wesleyan Church's Vision Statement

Spiritual Growth Tracker (cont.)

Take a look at where you are. What have you accomplished? These are steps you've already taken in your discipleship journey.

Now take a look at where you want to be in the next 6 months to 1 year. Whether your spiritual growth goal is the next stage or several stages ahead, be intentional about getting there. On the number lines below, read the question and circle the number that reflects how you feel*.

Is becoming more like Jesus important to you right now?

0	1	2	3	4	5
Nope	Not really	I don't know	Sort of	Yep	YES!

Do you have what you need to get to where you want to be?

0	1	2	3	4	5
Nope	Not really	I don't know	Sort of	Yep	YES!

Do you think you can get where you want to be?

0	1	2	3	4	5
Nope	Not really	I don't know	Sort of	Yep	YES!

1. Why is this goal important to you? _____

_____

2. What people, resources or skills do you need to get to your goal? _____

_____

3. Where can you find the support you listed in question 2? _____

_____

* Adapted from the Readiness Ruler, as used in Motivational Interviewing

What should I do with my life?

PART 5: MINISTRY

I'm made to serve God

Get to Know the Big Idea: Ministry

KNOW

Big Question: What should I do with my life?

Big Idea: I'm made to serve God

Bible Verse: "Each one should use whatever gift he has received to serve others." 1 Peter 4:10 NIV

Summer is probably one of the most fun times of the year. With no school or homework and great weather (most days), there's plenty of time to do whatever you want.

Sometimes, though, there can be too much time. Ever have a day when you have nothing to do and are bored out of your mind? It can be hard getting through days like that. They seem endless.

Can you imagine surviving a week like that? What about an entire year? Living without purpose is like that: Day after day of doing nothing that brings you joy. Getting frustrated because life feels pointless.

You probably wouldn't ever want that for yourself and God definitely doesn't want that for you. That's why he made you for a life of ministry. *Ministry* is service that's done out of love for God. It aims to share God's goodness with people. Ministry is one way God's family spreads his healing to the broken world. And believe it or not, you're designed to contribute in a special way!

THINK

Ministry in one place can look really different than ministry in another because of the diversity of people, places and needs in the world.

Come up with some creative ways to minister to kids where you live.

PRAY

Father God, I praise you because I'm wonderfully made. Help me to understand how you've made me. Show me how I can use what you've given me to share your love with others.

DO

God uniquely shapes everyone for a different purpose. Each person has an equal and important role to play.

1. Who are your 3 favorite heroes?

2. What's their "power"?

3. What are their roles in their community?

Gifts and Passions Shape Your Ministry

In the same way heroes accept their missions and use their gifts for the good of the world, when you accept your mission from God, you accept the spiritual gifts he gives you to help you fulfill your purpose.

Spiritual gifts are similar to a hero's gifts: they are special abilities you excel at without having to try very hard. They can be an action you do or a quality you have.

You use your gifts to help you fulfill your purpose. You find your purpose when you understand your *passions*. Passions are what you care most about. They can be people or things you could spend all day with.

When you use your spiritual gifts to invest in your passions so that you can serve others, you do ministry!

Big Question: What should I do with my life?

Big Idea: I'm made to serve God

Bible Verse: "Each one should use whatever gift he has received to serve others." 1 Peter 4:10 NIV

Passage: Acts 20:24 NIRV

"I want to complete the work the Lord Jesus has given me. He wants me to tell others about the good news of God's grace."

NOTES

_____

_____

_____

_____

_____

_____

_____

_____

_____

_____

_____

_____

_____

_____

_____

_____

_____

THINK

Understanding how God has gifted you and what your passions are will take time. It can be helpful to get the insight of people who know you well.

Ask your grown-up to give you clues about the gifts and passions they think you have. See if you can guess them.

PRAY

I'm excited that you have great plans in store for me, Lord! I look forward to serving you with the gifts and passions you've given me.

DO

What do you think your gifts and passions are? Take time to reflect on how you're shaped for ministry with the activity on the next page.

Spiritual Gifts and Passions Inventory

If you've already said "yes" to being part of God's family, you may already be developing your spiritual gifts. If not, God has them ready to go for when you are. This chapter's activity will help you think about how God has gifted you and the passions he's given you to pursue.

While this is a helpful start to understanding how you're shaped for ministry, it may take time for you to get a better idea of what your spiritual gifts are. One way to do that is by engaging in different opportunities. As you learn about various groups, environments, needs and resources, you'll get a feel for what you're especially good at and what you especially care for. This insight will help you understand and do ministry according to how God made you.

Spiritual Gifts
List 1–3 abilities or qualities you excel at. Make note of who you're with, where you are and when you use each gift. Circle all the reasons it's special to you.

1. _____

Who I'm with: _____

Where I am: _____

When I use it: _____

This spiritual gift is special to me because: I feel important using it

    I enjoy using it   I get to help someone   I have fun using it

    Other: _____

2. _____

Who I'm with: _____

Where I am: _____

When I use it: _____

This spiritual gift is special to me because: I feel important using it

    I enjoy using it   I get to help someone   I have fun using it

    Other: _____

Spiritual Gifts and Passions Inventory (cont.)

Spiritual Gifts (cont.)

3. _____

Who I'm with: _____

Where I am: _____

When I use it: _____

This spiritual gift is special to me because: I feel important using it

I enjoy using it   I get to help someone   I have fun using it

Other: _____

Passions

List 1–5 things you love or are really interested in. They can be things you could think about all day long; things you read, watch, sing and talk about; things you do without your grown-up asking or things you wish everyone loved as much as you do. Remember: There are no wrong answers!

1. _____

2. _____

3. _____

4. _____

5. _____

Interests can come and go with time. Passions are different; they are things you continue to care about even when you grow older, gain or lose friends, move to a new home or go through hard times.

Just like spiritual gifts, it'll take time to find out what matters most to you. Once you do, you'll look back and see that what you've gone through pointed to those passions!

Personality and Skills Shape Your Ministry

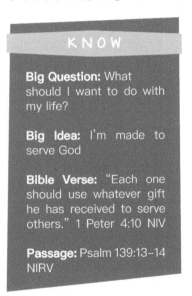

KNOW

Big Question: What should I want to do with my life?

Big Idea: I'm made to serve God

Bible Verse: "Each one should use whatever gift he has received to serve others." 1 Peter 4:10 NIV

Passage: Psalm 139:13–14 NIRV

Each superhero has a signature move. Their unique mix of personality and skills enables them to save the day in a way no other superhero can (and if anyone tries to copy, you can always tell!).

In the same way, God has made you with your own unique combination of personality and skills. Your *personality* is made up of your thoughts, feelings, qualities and behaviors. The *skills* you have are techniques, habits or abilities you know. This mix of personality and skills is, in part, what makes your signature move specific to just you. They help you do ministry in a way no one else can!

Learning how to use your personality and skills for God's kingdom work is a life–long process. It won't be a lonely one, though. Just as heroes receive guidance from a mentor and often work with others, you will, too--and you'll be at your best when you do.

"You put me together inside my mother's body. How you made me is amazing and wonderful. I praise you for that. What you have done is wonderful. I know that very well."

99

THINK

Personalities and skills differ from person to person--and the fact that you're different is a good thing!

1. What would happen if everyone was the same?

2. Name some differences between you and your grown-up. What makes differences a good thing?

PRAY

There's no one else like me! Thanks for making me one-of-a-kind, God. Make my heart big enough to appreciate the differences in your world.

DO

A smart guy named Socrates once said that the only life worth living is the one you take time to think about.

Take time to think and get to know yourself a little better on the next pages.

Personality and Skills Inventory

So many things make you unique: the color of your eyes, the shape of your fingerprint and the sound of your voice, to name just a few. The inventories in this chapter focus on two specific features: your personality and skills.

Personality

Your *personality* is the sum of who you are and how you act. Just as the sum in math is the total of an equation, your personality is the total of the parts that make you you:

Thoughts: what you think

Behaviors: what you do

Qualities: how you do it

Emotions: how you feel

Read through the statements* below and circle the option that sounds most like you. As you read, remember: There's no right or wrong quality. There's simply you, God-made and loved just the way you are.

What kind of setting gives you energy?
Some individuals enjoy being around people (extroversion) while others prefer to spend time alone (introversion). Although you'll face both situations in life, knowing which gives you more energy can help you recharge properly.

I have the most fun when:	I'm with a friend	I'm alone
I work best:	with a team	on my own
Being around people most of the time is:	exciting	exhausting
At the end of a long day, I want to:	relax with others	relax by myself
When I'm by myself,	I don't know what to do	I have plenty of ideas to keep busy
I seem to be more	extroverted	introverted

* These scales are adapted from the Myers–Briggs Type Indicator.

Personality and Skills Inventory (cont.)

How do you understand the world?

Some individuals like to stick to the facts and do what works (practical) while others prefer to explore rabbit holes and dream about where they lead (imaginative). Both types can be creative and productive. Knowing which you lean towards can set you up for success.

When I run into a problem,	I fix it right away	I think about how I can fix it
Coming up with lots of ideas	sounds like work	sounds like fun
Sticking to the facts	is easy	is hard
At the end of a movie, I talk about	what happened	what could have happened
I think about	what I can taste, touch, see, hear, feel	the possibilities
I seem to be more	practical	imaginative

How do you make decisions?

Some individuals make decisions based on *how* they can help (thinkers) while others make decisions based on *who* they can help (feelers). You'll likely do more of one and some of the other. Understanding how you make decisions can help you balance the choices you make, whether that's learning to do a little bit of both or asking someone for guidance.

Solutions should	be realistic	benefit others
My grown-up tells me I need to	be more considerate of others	be more thoughtful of consequences
I hope to be	fair to others	helpful to others
Good decisions	solve problems	make people feel important
I make choices based on	what makes sense	what I think others want
I seem to be more of a	thinker	feeler

Personality and Skills Inventory (cont.)

How do you get work done?
Some individuals like to make plans so they know what's next (fixed) while others prefer to make it up as they go (flexible). What makes these two types different is the level of certainty they need to feel comfortable. Understanding how much you need to know before you're comfortable starting a task can save you time (and headaches!) by getting you what you need from the get–go.

The best way to start a project is	with a plan	by jumping right in
I like it when	I know what's going to happen	I can do things whenever I want
When something changes unexpectedly,	I feel anxious	I feel intrigued
I'm good at	thinking ahead	thinking on the spot
Success feels like	getting the job done	going with the flow
I seem to be more	fixed	flexible

How do your surroundings affect you?
Some individuals are confident and unmoved by what others think (self–assured) while others are affected by what people have to say (self–critiquing). You'll feel both at different times, but one more than the other most of the time. Learn to trust yourself and what you can do. At the same time, remember that there's always room for growth.

When I mess up	I shrug it off; life goes on	I beat myself up about it
Most of the time, I do	what I want to do	what I think others want me to do
I believe I can do it	almost all the time	only sometimes
When someone is upset with me,	I don't worry too much about it	I can't stop worrying about it
I am the best me I can be	every day	some days
I seem to be more	self–assured	self–critiquing

Personality and Skills Inventory (cont.)

Now that you've got a better idea of what your personality is like, summarize it below by circling the option that best describes you:

I am someone who

Gets energy by being	with other people	on my own
Understands the world	through my senses	through my ideas
Makes decisions based on	what's needed	what helps others
Works best when	I have structure	I can take it at my own pace
Believes in myself	no matter what	when I get it right

And I am perfect the way I am!

Skills

Your *skills* are an additional feature that set you apart. They are techniques (like cooking), habits (like keeping a clean room) or abilities (like singing well). Some come naturally while others are learned. In either case, with the help of a trainer, teacher or program, you get a better grasp on how to use these skills.

There are millions of skills out there. They can be physical (using your body), mental (using your brain) and emotional (using your heart). The goal isn't to know every single skill; it's to know what you're good at and what you'll need help with. Write down your skills and circle the group to which it belongs. Then go back and count the number of skills in each group to determine where you're especially skilled. Knowing your strengths can help you figure out where and how you do ministry.

1. _____

       physical   mental   emotional

2. _____

       physical   mental   emotional

3. _____

       physical   mental   emotional

Personality and Skills Inventory (cont.)

4. _____

        physical   mental   emotional

5. _____

        physical   mental   emotional

6. _____

        physical   mental   emotional

7. _____

        physical   mental   emotional

Now think about the skills you don't yet know and want to learn. Write them down below and circle the group to which they belong.

1. _____

        physical   mental   emotional

2. _____

        physical   mental   emotional

3. _____

        physical   mental   emotional

4. _____

        physical   mental   emotional

Which group do most of your skills belong to? _____

Where can you learn the skills you don't yet know? _____

_____

Talk with your grown-up about how you can use these skills to minister to others and show them God's love.

Experiences Shape Your Ministry

Think about a time you felt really excited. What was happening? Now think about a time you felt lonely. What was happening then?

The things you go through are called *experiences*. They can be positive or negative; they can make you feel great or terrible. Chances are your life is made up of both experiences you've enjoyed and those you'd rather forget.

God uses experiences to shape you to become Christ-like. He also uses them to get you ready for ministry. The lessons you learn, the stories you collect and the way you grow through it all--those are all tools you'll need as you set out to show people God's love. God can use what you go through to bless others. Your willingness to serve him opens that door.

KNOW

Big Question: What should I do with my life?

Big Idea: I'm made to serve God

Bible Verse: "Each one should use whatever gift he has received to serve others." 1 Peter 4:10 NIV

Passage: Jeremiah 29:11 NIRV

"'I know the plans I have for you,' announces the Lord. 'I want you to enjoy success. I do not plan to harm you. I will give you hope for the years to come.'"

NOTES

_____

_____

_____

_____

_____

_____

_____

_____

_____

_____

_____

_____

_____

_____

_____

_____

_____

THINK

Having a wide variety of experiences helps you get a better idea of who you are and what you like. It also shows you what the world needs and ways to help.

Come up with a way to serve others based on what you've learned from your experiences.

PRAY

Father God, you fill my life with experiences that challenge me, teach me and change me. Give me courage to face each experience. Give me patience to wait and see how you're going to use them to bless others.

DO

Self-reflection is one way to get to know yourself better. A fun way to do that is through journaling.

Start your own self-reflection journal on the next page!

Reflecting on Experiences

Your life is full of experiences. Whether you enjoyed an experience or not, remember it or don't, God uses every one of them to shape you to serve others in a way no one else can.

For this activity, you'll reflect on 3–4 memories that stick out to you. God can work with good and bad situations, so these memories can be positive or negative. Write them down below, circle if it was a positive or negative experience and select the reason this experience is especially memorable.

1. _____

This was a   positive   /   negative   experience.

This experience is important to me because (check all that apply):

_____ I learned something new   _____ It wasn't what I expected

_____ I felt important   _____ I felt forgotten

_____ I felt loved   _____ I felt unloved

_____ I was with someone I love   _____ I was alone

_____ Other: _____

_____

2. _____

This was a   positive   /   negative   experience.

This experience is important to me because (check all that apply):

_____ I learned something new   _____ It wasn't what I expected

_____ I felt important   _____ I felt forgotten

_____ I felt loved   _____ I felt unloved

_____ I was with someone I love   _____ I was alone

_____ Other: _____

Reflecting on Experiences (cont.)

3. _____

This was a   positive   /   negative   experience.

This experience is important to me because (check all that apply):

_____ I learned something new   _____ It wasn't what I expected

_____ I felt important   _____ I felt forgotten

_____ I felt loved   _____ I felt unloved

_____ I was with someone I love   _____ I was alone

_____ Other: _____

_____

4. _____

This was a   positive   /   negative   experience.

This experience is important to me because (check all that apply):

_____ I learned something new   _____ It wasn't what I expected

_____ I felt important   _____ I felt forgotten

_____ I felt loved   _____ I felt unloved

_____ I was with someone I love   _____ I was alone

_____ Other: _____

_____

Now take a look through some of your most important memories. Talk about the questions below with your grown-up.

- What did you learn about yourself (gifts, passions, personality and skills) through these experiences?
- How have you grown by going through these experiences?
- What are some noteworthy experiences your grown-up has gone through?

DAY 33

What Service Looks Like

Big Question: What should I do with my life?

Big Idea: I'm made to serve God

Bible Verse: "Each one should use whatever gift he has received to serve others." 1 Peter 4:10 NIV

Passage: Galatians 5:13–14 NIRV

By now you know that God made you unique. No one has ever had or will ever again have your special combination of gifts, passions, personality, skills and experience.

If you think you're incredibly important because of how God's made you, you're right! God made you the way you are because the world needs what you can do. And that's exactly what he hopes happens: that you will be part of his plan to rescue the world––by being who you are and serving where you are.

Service is anything you do for anyone without asking for or expecting a reward. You serve because you see someone or something in need and you want to help by giving your time, energy or resources. There are lots of reasons to serve, but when you serve because you love God and want to show his love to others, you do ministry. Ministry happens at church, home, school or practice. The place doesn't matter; the reason why does.

"Serve one another in love. The whole law is fulfilled by obeying this one command. 'Love your neighbor as you love yourself.'"

The hardest part of serving might be learning to see needs. It's easy to think just about your own life and to forget about the needs of those around you.

How can you remind yourself each day to consider the needs of others?

PRAY

Jesus, you made me one of a kind! I love the way I am. Teach me how to love others the way I love myself, too. Show me how to serve you by serving others.

DO

Service doesn't have to be for people. If can be for nature, beliefs or non-living things.

By looking at how you spend your time, you can see what you serve most.

Given the option, what do you do more than anything else? If this is something that glorifies God, keep it up. If not, think of how to serve what matters to God.

DAY 34

The Power of Teamwork

It can be an incredible sight when people with different powers team up to fulfill a purpose. It's amazing to see in a movie and even more amazing to live out in real life.

God has given each of his children a special combination of powers. At the same time, no one has all the powers. This means there's a lot you can do on your own and even more you can do when you team up with others.

That's where being part of God's family comes in. You're surrounded by powerful people who love God. The possibilities for glorifying him and spreading his love are endless when you come together.

KNOW

Big Question: What should I do with my life?

Big Idea: I'm made to serve God

Bible Verse: "Each one should use whatever gift he has received to serve others." 1 Peter 4:10 NIV

Passage: Ecclesiastes 4:9–12 NIRV

"Two people are better than one. They can help each other in everything they do . . . One person could be overpowered. But two people can stand up for themselves."

112

_____
_____
_____
_____
_____
_____
_____
_____
_____
_____
_____
_____
_____
_____
_____
_____

THINK

Teams are made up of people who have various gifts, skills and personalities. The team is strongest when its members work together.

Talk about a time when being part of a team made a big difference in the outcome of an event.

PRAY

Lord God, thank you for all the creativity you put into making people unique. Help me to appreciate the ways others are different from me. Humble me so I can work with them.

DO

Knowing your strengths and areas for growth is important if you want to live a balanced life.

Think more about both these things on the next page.

Strengths and Areas for Growth

Strengths are things you do well or outstanding qualities you have. They can be used to help or hurt the world and the people in it. *Areas for growth* are things or qualities you have yet to learn or master. When you know what your strengths are, you can put them to good use. When you know what your areas for growth are, you're aware of when you might have to learn something new or ask for help.

List some of your strengths and areas for growth below. For each strength, write one way you can use it to help. For each area for growth, write one person who can help you when you're in need.

Strengths

1. _____

How I can use it to help: _____

_____

2. _____

How I can use it to help: _____

_____

3. _____

How I can use it to help: _____

_____

Areas for Growth

1. _____

Someone who can help: _____

2. _____

Someone who can help: _____

3. _____

Someone who can help: _____

Make the Big Idea Personal

KNOW

Big Question: What should I do with my life?

Big Idea: I'm made to serve God

Bible Verse: "Each one should use whatever gift he has received to serve others." 1 Peter 4:10 NIV

Maybe you're thinking you can't do it; ministry sounds too hard. You're not big enough. You don't have what you need. There's no one to help you. It's too scary.

But did you know? You're right where God wants you to be. There's no one better fit for your job than you!

You have what it takes to share his love with the world.

Any time you serve because you are loved by God and want to share his love with other people, you do ministry. Ministry gives people the opportunity to taste, touch, hear, see and feel the love of God. With that opportunity also comes the chance for God to give them the same chance he gave you: to say "yes" to being part of his family.

No one can do what you do. Will you serve God by being uniquely you?

115

THINK

Doing ministry can be intimidating, especially if you've never done it before.

When you think about serving others, what worries you?

PRAY

Lord, I want to be part of what you're doing. Give me insight into how you've made me. Show me how to love others using the unique qualities you've given me.

DO

Ministry can be long–term (lasting weeks to years) or short–term (lasting hours to weeks). It can be formal (with a program) or informal (on your own).

Brainstorm 3–5 ways you can engage in short–term ministry this month. Do one per week until you've done them all.

Short-Term Ministry Ideas

Come up with ideas for short-term ministry by thinking about the people you want to help. You can check out Appendix B for ideas. After you decide who you want to help, decide how you can help them and when you are going to do it. When you've completed the service, check it off your list.

☐ I want to help _____

by _____.

I will help on _____.

☐ I want to help _____

by _____.

I will help on _____.

☐ I want to help _____

by _____.

I will help on _____.

☐ I want to help _____

by _____.

I will help on _____.

☐ I want to help _____

by _____.

I will help on _____.

☐ I want to help _____

by _____.

I will help on _____.

How can my life make a difference?

PART 6: EVANGELISM

I'm made to do my part

Get to Know the Big Idea:
Evangelism

God's designed everything in your life--who you are, where you live, the family you have, your friends, the community around you--to work together towards a common end: evangelism.

Evangelism is telling people about God. Not just with words, though; with what's needed. Jesus often healed a person's sickness before he evangelized to them. He knew they needed to know he cared about them before they cared about anything he had to say. In the same way, you can use food, hugs, laughter and time (and many other things!) to start a conversation about God.

KNOW

Big Question: How can my life make a difference?

Big Idea: I'm made to do my part.

Bible Verse: "Be wise in the way you act toward outsiders; make the most of every opportunity." Colossians 4:5 NIV

Just like you came to know God through someone else's Christ-like example, others will come to know God through your own Christ-like example.

God's love has the power to heal, protect and transform lives. That's why he wants you to do your part to share it: so that as many people as possible can experience a full life on earth and an even fuller one in heaven.

_____

_____

_____

_____

_____

_____

_____

_____

_____

_____

_____

_____

_____

_____

_____

_____

THINK

Sometimes, actions speak louder than words because people can see evidence of what you believe.

Talk with your grown-up about a time someone's actions showed you how much they cared.

PRAY

Dear God, thank you for giving me a place in your family. You care about all the people you've created. But not all of them know you yet. I have a part in your plan to change that. Give me courage to evangelize.

DO

There are different ways to learn about God. Some are effective and make people want to know more about him. Others aren't; they make people want to avoid God.

Think some more about evangelism with the art activity on the next page.

122

Helpful Versus Harmful Evangelism

Helpful evangelism makes people want to know more about God. It can be transformational. Harmful evangelism makes them want to run away from God. It can be destructive. Brainstorm with your grown-up about what makes evangelism helpful and what makes it harmful.

When you've got an idea of how you can illustrate each type of evangelism, draw them below in the appropriate box. Then talk about whether you or your grown-up have experienced harmful evangelism. How did it affect the way you thought about God or his family?

Helpful Evangelism

Harmful Evangelism

Your Life Shows God's Love

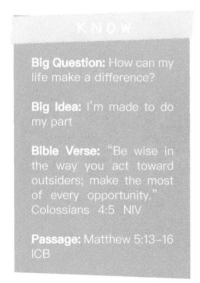

Big Question: How can my life make a difference?

Big Idea: I'm made to do my part

Bible Verse: "Be wise in the way you act toward outsiders; make the most of every opportunity." Colossians 4:5 NIV

Passage: Matthew 5:13–16 ICB

Sharing God's love begins with meeting needs: giving encouraging words, sharing a meal, spending time together. Learning to pay attention so you can see and meet needs helps you build relationships. Those relationships are an opportunity to earn trust and eventually share the whole story of God's love.

Sharing the whole story of God's love takes time. There are different parts to include. You can share your *testimony*. This is the story about how you met God and decided to be part of his family.

You can share *lessons* that God has taught you. These are important things you've learned about what it means to live as a Christian. You can talk about your *passions* and how God has shaped you to help people in a unique way.

You can share the *gospel* (found in "The Beginning") and encourage people to respond by saying, "Yes!" to being God's child, too. Whatever approach you use, evangelize because you love God and people so much you want them to love God, too.

"Be a light for other people. Live so that they will see the good things you do. Live so that they will praise your Father in heaven."

124

When it comes to sharing God's love, remember to follow Jesus' lead: show love more than you talk about it. The more people feel you care, the more likely they'll listen to what you have to say.

1. Who cares about you?

2. How do you know they care?

God, I thank you that there's healing for the brokenness in the world. That healing is found in your son, Jesus. Open my eyes to see every chance I have to share this good news with others.

Practice telling your testimony by answering the questions below:

1. How did you learn about God?

2. What made you want to be part of his family?

3. What's God helping you with right now?

A Kid's Secret Weapon

Sometimes it may feel like you can't do much because you're a kid. Sometimes it might feel like only adults get to do important things. Sometimes, though, a kid is exactly what God needs to make a big difference.

Jesus says kids are most important in God's kingdom (Matt. 18:2–6). There's something special about you *right now*, something that comes more easily to you than to grown-ups. It's got something to do with your heart (Mk. 10:13–16).

More than once in the Bible, God uses children to show his love (see Appendix C). He sees your desire to help, your interest in others and your humility to learn what you don't yet know. He wants to use those wonderful qualities to spread his healing love to the world. You can do important things as a kid!

KNOW

Big Question: How can my life make a difference?

Big Idea: I'm made to do my part.

Bible Verse: "Be wise in the way you act toward outsiders; make the most of every opportunity." Colossians 4:5 NIV

Passage: 1 Tim. 4:12 NIRV

"Don't let anyone look down on you because you are young. Set an example for the believers in what you say and in how you live. Also set an example in how you love and in what you believe. Show the believers how to be pure."

NOTES

_____

_____

_____

_____

_____

_____

_____

_____

_____

_____

_____

_____

_____

_____

_____

_____

_____

THINK

All grown-ups were kids once upon a time. They likely had dreams about how they wanted to make a difference in the world.

1. Ask your grown-up to share their childhood dream.

2. What's your dream for yourself?

PRAY

I'm made to make a difference as a kid. What an honor, Lord! Remind me that size and age don't stop you from using me to do big things.

DO

Kids have done some incredible things! Look them up online:

– Thomas Gregory and the English Channel

– Robby Novak, Kid President

– Gitanjali Rao, STEAM Squad

– Savanna Karmue, Happy Heart Advice

DAY 39

Balance: the Secret Ingredient

When it comes to taking care of yourself, it's not only knowing what you need but also *how much* of it you need. Keeping your brain, heart and body in good health ultimately requires balance.

In this case, *balance* is having the right *amount* of the right *activities* and *people* in your life. Too much of one thing or not enough of another can be harmful.

God's made you to enjoy him (worship), be part of his family (fellowship), become like Jesus (discipleship), serve others (ministry) and tell them about his love (evangelism); but he wants you to go about all of that with balance, taking care of yourself and others on the way.

You can keep your life balanced in different ways:
1. Spend time with people you love; share your triumphs and struggles with them
2. Ask for prayer and pray for others
3. Reflect on where you've been, where you are, where you want to be and how you can get from one place to another
4. Ask for guidance and help; you're not alone!
5. Teach others what you know and learn from them what you don't

THINK

Your body is designed to tell you when your life is out of balance. Your brain notices first and tells the rest of your body. Then your body responds to the imbalance.

What happens to your body when life is out of balance?

Visit Appendix D for more on your body's responses to imbalance.

PRAY

Honestly, Father, finding balance isn't always fun (like eating veggies!). It's life–giving, though: it energizes me and keeps my brain, heart and body well. Discipline me to fight for balanced living.

DO

Balance looks different from person to person; you're each different, after all.

Take time to think about how you can create balance in your life. The activity on the next pages can guide you.

NOTES

The Great Balancing Act

Life is full of people and activities. Some of them you enjoy and others you don't. Imagine a balance scale (pictured below). When your life is balanced, the amount of energy you have is equal to the amount of energy it takes for your work (in this case, your work is interacting with the people and completing the activities in your life).

When it's not, you have too much of one (energy) or the other (work). Life unbalanced can make you feel antsy, frustrated or stuck. If life gets too unbalanced, it can even cause your brain, heart or body to break.

The people and activities you enjoy *give* energy. This is your body's way of telling you that those things are making positive changes in your health. Try to do something on this list at least once a day. Whenever you're feeling irritated, unsafe or tired, definitely use this list for ideas on how to turn your day around.

The people and activities you don't enjoy *take* energy. This is your body's way of telling you that your brain, heart or body require extra effort to get through these situations. While they may not be enjoyable, they often give you opportunities to improve the way you think, speak and act.

If possible, avoid spending too much time with people or activities that take a lot of energy (you'll get cranky and get everyone else cranky). If you can't avoid it, bring along something to do that gives you energy. Take breaks as you work to re-energize and get your scale balanced again.

At times you'll get do what you love; at other times, you'll have to do what you don't. Knowing what gives and takes your energy helps you keep balanced by allowing you to plan. You can make time for what gives you energy and prepare ahead of time for what drains it.

The Great Balancing Act (cont.)

On the balance scale below, list 3–5 activities that energize you and 3–5 activities that wear you out.

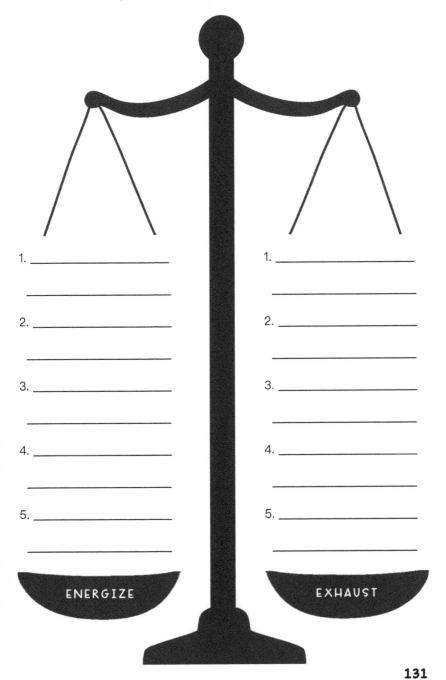

1. _____

_____

2. _____

_____

3. _____

_____

4. _____

_____

5. _____

_____

ENERGIZE

1. _____

_____

2. _____

_____

3. _____

_____

4. _____

_____

5. _____

_____

EXHAUST

DAY 40

Find Your Reason

You're at a time in your life where you're learning how to live in the world around you by watching the people most important to you. They're showing you different ways to live and the consequences--good and bad--that come with their decisions. Over time, you'll form values that influence the way you think, speak and act.

Values are your beliefs about what is important. They answer the six questions you explored in this book (find them on page vii). Your answers to these questions determine why you do the things you do.

KNOW

Big Question: How can my life make a difference?

Big Idea: I'm made to do my part.

Bible Verse: "Be wise in the way you act toward outsiders; make the most of every opportunity." Colossians 4:5 NIV

When your answers line up with God's answers, you unlock one of the most precious treasures ever: God–honoring *purpose*: an eternal reason to live with joy, even as a broken kid in a broken world. God's love will shine through your thoughts, words and actions. It will bring healing and hope. It will make a difference, all because you said, "yes" to God.

NOTES

_____

_____

_____

_____

_____

_____

_____

_____

_____

_____

_____

_____

_____

_____

_____

_____

_____

THINK

Those you admire likely have a clear purpose: They know who they are and how they want to help others.

1. Name someone you admire.

2. What kind of person are they?

3. How do they help others?

PRAY

God, thank you for this journey. I'm grateful for all the things I have learned. Now guide me and surround me with supporters so I can live as a kid on purpose.

DO

You've got a head full of new knowledge. The best way to use it? By doing what you've learned!

Figure out your values and write your answers to the Big Questions on the next pages.

My Values

What you believe to be important is called a *value*. Values can be beliefs about things such as:
- **People** (example: you believe family is important),
- **Places** (example: you believe nature is important),
- **Things** (example: you believe your belongings are important),
- **Practices** (example: you believe going to school is important)
- **Qualities** (example: you believe being kind is important)

This activity helps you figure out some of your most important values. It also helps you see if they match God's values or not.

Start by listing 3–5 things you believe are very important (so important you wish everyone else believed them, too):

1. _____

2. _____

3. _____

4. _____

5. _____

On the next page is a values bracket. It'll help you prioritize your values (that's just a fancy way of saying it'll show you how important each value is compared to the others). You'll use numbers to identify each value. For example, the value you listed on line 1 is represented by "1," the value you listed on line 2 is represented by "2" and so on.

A bracket connects a pair of values (that's the line that goes up from one number, across and down to the other number). Between the two connected values, choose the one you think is more important. Write it in the empty box that stems from the bracket.

Do this with each pair of values and work your way up the pyramid. The number you write in at the top is the value that's most important to you.

Work your way back down the pyramid. Each line will have a number that isn't listed in the line above it. That's the next most important value. The values most important to you will be at the top of the pyramid and the less important ones will be at the bottom. You can re-write your values in order of priority below the pyramid (give your values new numbers based on their importance).

For fun, ask your grown-up to complete this activity, as well. Compare your values. What do you have in common and what's different?

My Values (cont.)

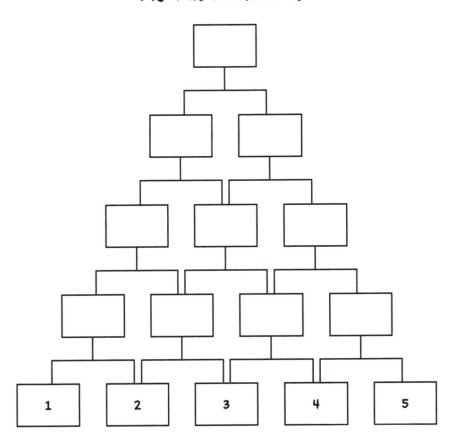

Prioritized Values

1. _____

2. _____

3. _____

4. _____

5. _____

These values are really important to you. When you stick with them, you'll feel at peace. When you don't, you might feel uneasy. Part of being a Christian is exploring what *people* (yourself included) say is important, comparing it to what *God* says is important and learning how to value what God values. There will be times your values match up with God's and times they don't.

My Values (cont.)

When your values or the values others are asking you to believe in don't match up with God's, that's a sign to pause. Ask yourself:

- "What do I value and what does God value?"
- "What's the difference between our values?"
- "What has to change for my value to match God's?"

If you ever find yourself wondering what God values, the best place to look for answers is the Bible. Here are some things he says about the values listed at the beginning of this activity:

- **People – Philippians 2:3–4 ICB**
  "When you do things, do not let selfishness or pride be your guide. Be humble and give more honor to others than to yourselves. Do not be interested only in your own life, but be interested in the lives of others."

- **Places – Deuteronomy 10:14 NIRV**
  "The heavens belong to the Lord your God. Even the highest heavens belong to him. He owns the earth and everything in it."

- **Things – Luke 6:38 ICB**
  "Give, and you will receive. You will be given much. It will be poured into your hands—more than you can hold. You will be given so much that it will spill into your lap. The way you give to others is the way God will give to you."

- **Practices – Romans 14:12 NIRV**
  "We will all have to explain to God the things we have done."

- **Qualities – Galatians 5:22–23 ICB**
  "But the Spirit gives love, joy, peace, patience, kindness, goodness, faithfulness, gentleness, self–control. There is no law that says these things are wrong."

Take time to make sure what's important to you is also important to God. When your values match up with God's, you'll live out your purpose automatically: true worship, fellowship, discipleship, ministry and evangelism will transform your thoughts, words and actions so that you glorify God in all you do.

My Purpose Statement

What will the Big Ideas look like in your life? Each person will live them out differently, and those differences are what spread the good news of God's love even further.

Write down your response to each question. Make copies of it and hang them up around your house so that when you feel lost, confused or undecided, you can see it and be reminded of your purpose.

What am I doing here?

_____

_____

What does God want from me?

_____

_____

Where do I belong?

_____

_____

What kind of person do I want to be?

_____

_____

What will I do with my life?

_____

_____

How can my life make a difference?

_____

_____

WHAT NOW?

You've come to the end of the book, but your journey as a kid on purpose is just beginning. You've learned a lot in the last 40 days. Don't worry about remembering everything. You can always come back if you need a reminder about your purpose and place in this world.

What you do need to remember are these two things:

> 1. Love God with your thoughts, words and actions. Love him with your time, energy and resources.

and then,

> 2. Do what matters most to you. When you love God first, he guides the rest of your life so that you show his love wherever you are, whatever you're doing.

You can do this. You can make a difference, kiddo.

APPENDIX A

Christ-like Printables

Color and cut out these printables along the dotted line. Then tape them up or leave them around your house to use as visual reminders to be Christ-like with your thoughts, words and actions. Great areas to place these cards include the bathroom, your bedside table and your backpack.

I can be Christ-like

I can be Christ-like

APPENDIX B

Ministry Ideas

A simple definition of ministry is service that's meant to 1) show God's love by 2) helping someone other than yourself. Ministry can also be known as "service projects" or "outreach events."

Ministry begins with an understanding of God's great love for you and the blessings that come with being part of his family. This knowledge is so exciting you don't want to keep it to yourself--so you don't! You go and share with others about God's love in the best way possible: by showing it.

God showed love for you when he gave you what you needed: a chance to become part of his family and be healed from brokenness. You can follow God's example of loving others by meeting people's needs, too. When considering how to minister to someone, ask yourself, "What does that person need?" and "How can I help meet that need?"

Here are some examples of ways to minister to various needs:
- Create a themed (arts & crafts, board games, family movie night, etc.) care basket for neighbors (remember to include a Bible verse)
- Bring baked goodies to a local public safety unit (fire station, police precinct, post office, etc.)
- Treat a family to an all-day access pass to a zoo or theme park
- Pick up trash around your neighborhood
- Provide dinner for someone going through a hard time
- Pack and distribute hygiene bags (toothpaste, toothbrush, tissues, lip balm, soap, snacks, etc.) for the homeless, whether in person or at a shelter
- Help your neighbor with yard work
- Pack a Christmas shoebox and share the gospel with kids around the world through Samaritan's Purse
- Start a canned food drive at your school, in your neighborhood or at church
- Host a school supply drive and donate proceeds to students or teachers
- Volunteer at or donate to an animal shelter
- Plant trees in your backyard or through a local organization
- Make thank-you cards or gifts for community workers (refuse workers, mail carriers, government employees, etc.)
- Spend time with the elderly at a retirement home
- Support an animal through the World Wildlife Fund's Symbolic Species Adoptions
- Donate eyewear you no longer need to programs such as VSP's Eyes of Hope
- Collect toiletries and beauty products for a women's shelter
- Design encouraging centerpieces for an assisted living facility
- Share books through Little Free Library
- Give a village access to water, livestock or gardening resources through Heifer International
- Sponsor a child's well-being through Compassion International

APPENDIX C

Children in the Bible

Age doesn't stop God from using you! Here are some kids from the Bible who said, "Yes!" to being used for God's purpose.

Miriam

Miriam was big sister to Moses. She made sure he survived in a time baby boys were being killed by the pharaoh. Moses eventually freed God's people from slavery in Egypt.

A Slave Girl

Naaman had a slave girl (whose family he likely killed). Leprosy destroyed his body. She helped him recover by telling him where to find a prophet who could ask God to heal him.

Samuel

As a child, Samuel received a vision from God about how God would discipline the priest's sons for blasphemy. Samuel then told the priest, who understood and accepted God's decision.

A Generous Boy

There was a boy who willingly shared his lunch of two fish and five loaves of bread. His generosity (along with prayer!) fed more than 5,000 people who had gathered to listen to Jesus teach.

APPENDIX D

Bodily Signs of Imbalance

God's made it so that your body tells you when it needs something. These signs can be organized into many categories. Some of the most common categories are: mental (having to do with your thoughts), emotional (having to do with your moods), physical (having to do with your body) and social (having to do with your relationships).

Although researchers can't say that everyone responds to imbalance in the same way, they can say that many people do. Below are examples of how your thoughts, moods, body and relationships can be affected by imbalance. Circle or highlight responses you go through when you're having a hard time.

When you experience these signs for a few days in a row, your body is telling you it's out of balance. Ask yourself, "How has my regular schedule changed?" Take note of the differences; they are what's causing the imbalance. Then use a coping skill (found on the next page) to help you deal with what you're going through.

Mental Signs of Imbalance	
You have trouble focusing	You worry a lot
You can't remember things	You have too many thoughts too fast
You feel guilty	You lose interest in your hobbies

Emotional Signs of Imbalance	
You cry often	Your moods change quickly
You feel cranky	You have panic attacks
You don't want to do anything	You feel hopeless

Physical Signs of Imbalance	
You're often tired	You don't have energy
You feel restless or antsy	You have trouble sleeping
You eat too much or too little	You lose movement abilities

Social Signs of Imbalance	
You avoid people you care about	You depend on someone too much
You resent people you care about	You need someone's approval
You criticize or blame others	You are unable to treat others kindly

Regaining Control and Restoring Balance

Everyone experiences imbalance. It's a part of life in a broken world. Not everyone knows how to cope with it, though. *Coping* is the process of dealing with an issue in a healthy way. When you cope with the signs you circled on the previous page, you regain control and restore balance to your heart, mind, body and soul.

Below are examples of easy-to-learn coping skills. Use these methods to regain control whenever you begin to feel as though you're losing power over your thoughts, words and actions. Circle or highlight the ones you'd like to try.

When I feel imbalanced, I can:

Read a book	Take a nap	Hang out with a friend
Sit in silence	Play with slime	Take a walk outside
Scream into my pillow	Suck on a mint	Talk to a grown-up
Smell the grass	Punch a stuffed animal	Color a picture
Cuddle in a blanket	Take a shower	Spend time alone
Wash my hands slowly	Hug myself tightly	Take deep breaths
Write down my thoughts	Pray for myself	Play with a pet
Take a break	Sing as loud as I can	Count to 100 by 2's
Go for a swim	Lie out in the sun	Paint a picture
Do stretches	Bury my feet in sand	Squeeze a ball
Ask for help	Listen to music	Clean my room
Dance until I'm happy	Run across the yard	Find 5 yellow things
Play a board game	Jump for 2 minutes	Ride my bike

Sarah Her has worked with kids ever since she was a kid herself. She studied ministry for children, youth and families in college and pursued graduate studies in counseling in thereafter. When she's not building forts or playing board games, she writes about practical, wholehearted adulting on her blog. You can join her in living un-stuck at www.herwildernesscreated.com.